OEPKE NOORDMANS

THE HISTORICAL SERIES OF THE REFORMED CHURCH IN AMERICA
NO. 78

OEPKE NOORDMANS
Theologian of the Holy Spirit

Karel Blei

Translated by Allan J. Janssen

WILLIAM B. EERDMANS PUBLISHING COMPANY
Grand Rapids, Michigan / Cambridge, UK

Wm. B. Eerdmans Publishing Co.
2140 Oak Industrial Drive SE, Grand Rapids, Michigan 49503
PO Box 163, Cambridge CB3 9PU UK
www.eerdmans.com

Printed in the United States of America

Library of Congress Cataloging-in-Publication Data

Blei, Karel.
    Oepke Noordmans : theologian of the holy spirit / Karel Blei ;
Translated by Allan J. Janssen.
    pages cm -- (The historical series of the Reformed Church in America
; 78)
  Includes bibliographical references and index.
   ISBN 978-0-8028-7085-8 (pbk. : alk. paper) 1. Noordmans, Oepke,
1871-1956. I. Title.
  BX9479.N66B54 2013
  230'.42092--dc23
                              2013005465

This volume is made possible through the gracious support of

Stichting Zonneweelde
RDO Balije van Utrecht - Vicariefonds
Dr. M. van Wichenstichting
Christiana Maria Stichting

The Historical Series of the Reformed Church in America

The series was inaugurated in 1968 by the General Synod of the Reformed Church in America acting through the Commission on History to communicate the church's heritage and collective memory and to reflect on our identity and mission, encouraging historical scholarship which informs both church and academy.

www.rca.org/series

General Editor
> Rev. Donald J. Bruggink, PhD, DD
> Western Theological Seminary
> Van Raalte Institute, Hope College

Associate Editor
> George Brown Jr., PhD
> Western Theological Seminary

Copy Editor
> Laurie Baron

Production Editor
> Russell L. Gasero

Commission on History
> James Hart Brumm, MDiv, Blooming Grove, New York
> Douglas Carlson, PhD, Northwestern College, Orange City, Iowa
> David M. Tripold, PhD, Monmouth University
> Audrey Vermilyea, Bloomington, Minnesota
> Matthew Van Maastricht, MDiv, Milwaukee, Wisconsin
> Linda Walvoord, PhD, University of Cincinnati

Contents

Why Noordmans for America?

Paul R. Fries

Book titles in the interrogative are currently fashionable. The title promises an answer to the question it poses: *Why Catholicism Matters, Why Children Matter, Why Orwell Matters*—the Amazon listings go on and on, page after page. And while these repetitive titles may seem unimaginative and even tedious, there is something direct and honest about them. To ask whether the subject of a book is worth its cost and the effort of reading is clearly appropriate. The question is of course rhetorical: were the author not convinced of the book's relevance it would not have been written. Obviously Karel Blei, author of *Oepke Noordmans: Theologian of the Spirit*, believes in the importance of Noordmans's thought and so does the book's translator, Allan Janssen. Anyone with even a smattering of knowledge of Dutch theology written in the second half of the twentieth century will understand Blei's conviction. It is unlikely that there was a single theologian of significance writing during this enormously productive period who was not in one way or another influenced by Noordmans. Why Noordmans is relevant to Dutch readers is self-evident.

This is not the case, however, when the intended audience is American. The theological giants writing in the Netherlands in the post-World War II decades are known only by a few men and women in the United States and Canada attuned to the theological world in Holland. The question of why a book on the life and thought of this little known Dutch theologian is relevant to the faith and practice of the Christian church in North America, even of Protestant churches with roots in the Netherlands, is *not* self-evident.

The question is actually twofold. Even if the relevance of Noordmans for an American theological audience can be demonstrated, one may still ask why the Commission on History of the Reformed Church in America (RCA) would elect to publish this monograph. The commission's stated purpose is "...to communicate the church's heritage and collective memory and to reflect on our identity and mission, encouraging historical scholarship which informs both church and academy." While at first glance, a study of Noordmans does not seem to answer to any of these stipulations, a closer look suggests that it does. There are good if not obvious reasons for the commission to sponsor this book. The key words in this regard are "identity and mission." In an indirect at twice remove, Noordmans in fact has influenced the understanding of mission and factored into the theological self-identity of the denomination.

I say in an indirect at twice removed manner because with a few exceptions Noordmans's thought as indicated above is largely unknown to theologians, both in the pastorate and the academy, of the RCA. Yet Noordmans has been a factor in the theological discourse of the denomination over the past decades, not by direct interaction but through the Dutch theologians he influenced. One thinks of, among others, the writings of C.G. Berkouwer, Hendrikus Berkhof, and particularly A.A. van Ruler. An archeology of such influence is beyond the scope of this foreword; it is enough to indicate here that the RCA's engagement of liturgy, theology, order, and ethics since the 1960s has been illuminated by interaction with Dutch theologians and thus by the thought of Noordmans.

While those interested in Dutch theology will find Blei's account of Noordmans's life and theological development helpful, the importance of this book extends beyond the presumably narrow readership. It is the content of Noordmans's thought—bold, sometimes startling, always insightful, and occasionally troubling—that makes this book richly worthy of attention. One may find, as he or she ponders Noordmans's teachings, a new perspective on and deepened grasp of various subjects of theological concern, e.g., predestination, the incarnation, eschatology, and, most profoundly, the action of the Holy Spirit. And one may also find in Noordmans a corrective for the unimaginative and superficial treatment of these and other subjects in the popular life of the church. Noordmans's theology is surprisingly original and at the same time always critical and substantive.

Readers familiar with the centuries-long debates over predestination in Reformed circles may be surprised, for example, by Noordmans's suggestion that this doctrine does not speak of eternal decrees but of spiritual awareness, a consciousness of both moral failure and divine grace, a divine grace that in fact shatters our efforts to achieve morality, throwing us radically on the will of God. Traditional Calvinism would find shocking, even scandalous, the idea that election is the opposite of morality, that our efforts to lead moral lives are exploded by the doctrine. But this, Noordmans teaches, is its fundamental meaning. Predestination testifies to God's preference for sinner and divine abhorrence of human moral constructs. If Roman Catholic social theory as popularized by liberation theology can speak of the Bible's preferential option for the poor, Noordmans can proclaim God's preferential choice of the sinner. In a wonderful statement he asserts, "God (is) so mild in the forgiveness of guilt that it offends us."

Noordmans's teaching on creation and recreation is also intriguing. In his most systematic work, *Herschepping*, he employs the notions of creation and recreation as foci of a comprehensive theological statement. Creation, according to Noordmans, is not formation but separation, not shaping but dividing. Genesis 1 does not depict God as a kind of divine potter, shaping primal matter into harmonious forms, but rather as one who by Word and Spirit engages in cosmic separation; light is separated from darkness, heaven from earth, land from water, man from woman. Each act of separation is a divine judgment, and the result of each judgment in pre-lapsarian creation is another judgment: "...and it was good." In the post-lapsarian history recorded in the Old Testament, God continues to render judgment, separating good from evil, justice from injustice, truth from lies, mercy from cruelty. But now a new factor has entered creation: human freedom. Thus God continues to create, separating fallen creation from the new creation manifested in the Spirit-mediated resurrected Christ. Thus it is by separation, by God's judgments, that the consummation is given a place in history. Noordmans speaks of creation as a spot of light surrounding the cross— the light of Christ the *nova creatio* who makes all things new.

It is, however, in Noordmans's doctrine of the Holy Spirit that the most experimental and possibly disconcerting dynamics of his theology appear. Here, I believe, we find the most compelling response to the question, why Noordmans? Blei has subtitled his book *Theologian of the Holy Spirit* for good reason. If Abraham Kuyper's ponderous work on the Holy Spirit surveys the terrain of Reformed thought on the Spirit, Oepke Noordmans's *Gestalte en Geest* offers an expedition into uncharted territories. *Geest* translates simply as Spirit, but the English rendering of *gestalte* is far more complicated. By it Noordmans means an entity having meaning. Abraham, Moses, Saul, and David are all such *gestalten*. They are figures who serve to formulate the faith and practice of Israel. Rather than a vision of the Spirit employing these *gestalten* to build on one another, as stones in a stairs leading to an apex, the incarnation and Jesus Christ, Noordmans contends that the Spirit *shatters* each, so that a new *gestalte* can be formed. Here again Noordmans introduces the notion of separation; the Spirit and the presence and power of the new creation are dissolved so new configurations drawn by the new creation can come into existence.

Even Jesus is such a *gestalte* to be shattered. The understanding of the resurrected Christ in the mind of his disciples before Pentecost is negated by the Spirit. This is certainly one of Noordmans's most controversial teachings. It leads him to see in the Book of Acts a swerve away from the Christology of the apostles toward a Christology of the Spirit. The appointment of the seven deacons, including Stephen, to serve the Greek Christians signals a break with the twelve apostles' understanding of the gospel. It is Paul, however, who is the great agent and interpreter of the Spirit's destruction of the *gestalte* initially embraced by the apostles. It is he who successfully challenges the early Christian Judaizers when, for example, he confronts Peter over the necessity of circumcision. The pastoral letter issued by the Council of Jerusalem represents the new *gestalte* emerging from the deconstruction of the old. The Spirit divides, shatters, and reconfigures, and so does the new creation assume *gestalten* in time and space. As Blei writes, Noordmans's motto is "Paul comes and Peter goes." For Paul, who wrote the earliest books of the New Testament, it is not Jesus who gives us the Spirit, but the Spirit who gives us Jesus.

My hope is that by offering this glimpse of three facets of Noordmans's fascinating thought I have suggested why Americans might want to read Noordmans. Yet the brief discussion above, intended to prick readers' interest, have only touched the surface of the eccentric Dutch pastor's brilliant theology. It should not be thought, however, that his original and imaginative re-visioning of the Christian faith is limited to predestination, creation/recreation, and the Holy Spirit. Noordmans's study of Augustine remains relevant not because of its historical scholarship, but because of its deep reflections on church and empire—for Augustine the Roman Empire, for Noordmans the looming specter of the Third Reich, for us the perhaps more vexing problem of the church-friendly American Empire. One is also impressed by Noordmans's penetrating theology of liturgy, with its attention to Word and sacrament—these discussions alone are worth the price of the book.

Oepke Noordmans, although a theological celebrity in his later years, never left the parish ministry and never wrote a book or essay, or delivered a lecture, intended for academe. He was a servant of the congregation and the larger church. His profound theology developed in response to the concerns of both. It then seems fitting that the author of this lucid presentation of Noordmans's theology also found his theological vocation apart from the academy. Karel Blei has also been a servant of the church, both local and national (and international). And while now on the faculty roster as a part-time professor at New Brunswick Theological Seminary, the same is largely true of the book's translator, Allan Janssen. Janssen has presented an excellent rendering of not only Blei's text, but also of the difficult quotations from the writings of Noordmans. It is encouraging to know that there are still men and women in the pastoral ministry who not only take an interest in theology, but who also participate enthusiastically in the theological enterprise. We are indebted to Blei, Janssen, the Commission on History of the RCA, and yes, Oepke Noordmans, for the work that follows.

CHAPTER 1

Introduction

There is little that seems remarkable in the events that constitute Oepke Noordmans's life. Born (in 1871) and raised in Friesland, he studied theology in Leiden and Utrecht. His student years were long and difficult, interrupted as they were by illness. Consequently, he did not become a village preacher in the Reformed Church until 1903, at the age of thirty-two. He remained a preacher his entire life, first in Friesland and later in the Achterhoek, until his retirement in 1943 following forty years of ministry. Throughout his life he played a formidable role in the Netherlands Reformed Church, both in the years of his active ministry and then until his death in 1956. I will sketch his life and thought rather briefly in this introduction.

Coming from a milieu stamped by both the Réveil and the Ethical Movement, Noordmans was from the outset an outspoken representative of ethical theology, with its emphasis on the mutuality of the Word and the human heart. Early on, he emphasized the "humane" character of Christian truth. He soon developed as a speaker and writer, active in regional and provincial affairs.

1

Early on, he showed interest in the particular significance of the preacher's task as minister of the Word. Personal experiences as a minister in a congregation made him all the more sensitive to the role and function of the preacher in a congregation. Consequently, he became one of the founders of the Covenant of Netherlands Preachers, who were passionate not only for an improved legal position for preachers but also for a more spiritual vision of the essence of the office of minister of the Word.

In the 1920s he took particular note of the significance of the theology of Karl Barth, in which the concentration on the religious personality was transcended. He was among those who introduced Barth in the Netherlands. He did so through lectures, articles, and publications. Barth's new theological efforts tallied with the critical turn that Noordmans's own theology made at about the same time. In that context he also reflected critically on the development and future of ethical theology. He did not hide his own growing reservations about Barth. But Noordmans's criticism emerged from a deep relationship. He saw the consequences for Barthian theology which lay even beyond Barth's own view. That made for a critique of exceptional content.

Noordmans was later involved in the pre-World War II struggle for the renewal of the Netherlands Reformed Church. His contribution was inspired by a deep knowledge of the church fathers (Augustine) and reformers (Calvin) and rare insight into what was philosophically relevant (Descartes, Kant). At the same time he was engaged, along with others of his theological ilk, in important discussions with the followers of Abraham Kuyper and neo-Calvinism.

Noordmans's interest was not in intraecclesial bickering. At issue was the question of the meaning of Christian faith itself and the continuation of the church at a time overshadowed by the rise of National Socialism. The threat that emerged and became real when the Second World War broke out and involved the Netherlands should not and could not, in his opinion, remain absent from theological reflection. In those years Noordmans felt as though he were a walker along the shore at the rising tide. Such a walker cannot continue his course as before; he must change course.

Others were also engaged in church renewal, sometimes in ways that evoked critical questions from Noordmans. That was the case with the Liturgical Movement. Noordmans found himself challenged to take a position. He engaged in a high-level discussion with the religious historian G. van der Leeuw. Liturgy appears to have been more than a question of aesthetics or style for Noordmans, but represented a particular starting point, and he put precisely that on the agenda as a matter for discussion. The discussion included the question of the ecumené, and it was taken up again following the war.

In the prewar years, Noordmans became more and more a person of original and personal authority. Attempts to appoint him ecclesiastical professor, undertaken in 1926 and 1934, failed as a result of church politics and so he remained an "ordinary" village preacher; that failure, however, did nothing to diminish his authority. He received official recognition of his extraordinary merits when the University of Groningen gave him an honorary doctorate in theology in 1935.

During and following the Second World War, the renewal of the Netherlands Reformed Church continued. Noordmans had been involved in that struggle for a long time, but he could not always agree without reservation with the course that it took. He had his doubts about the theology of the apostolate, so dominant in those years. Was not the faith thereby in danger of being reduced to action? A discussion with H. Kraemer, the leader of *Gemeenteopbouw*[1] also began over these matters.

In the final, postwar, period of his life, he remained influential, primarily through his many meditations, a series written for the periodical, *In de Waagschaal*. Noordmans later collected and published them himself in book form. His theology in this period bore the stamp of the war years, which had been particularly difficult for Noordmans. In the meditations he developed his thought further, almost incidentally, as it were, through reflections on biblical texts. It meant the completion of a theology almost peculiar to him, in which the work of the Holy Spirit is placed at center. The meditations were at the same time a form of pastoral work, by which many people were heartened and encouraged. The meditations, like Noordmans's entire work, remain fascinating and stimulating.

For that reason, he has remained a subject of study into the present. There is a steady stream of publications on Noordmans. Very soon after his death, plans originated for the publication of his collected works. However, it took a few decades before that publication began. The first volume appeared in 1978. In 2004—later than originally intended—the tenth and final volume was presented. Carefully arranged and accompanied by notes and indexes, the entire work is available for all.

---

[1]   [Trans. The term *gemeenteopbouw*, literally "building up of the congregation" will be left untranslated. Along with *Kerkherstel* and *Kerkopbouw*, it denotes an important movement in the Netherlands Reformed Church in the 1930s and 1940s.]

This fact alone is reason for further study of Noordmans. The Noordmans Foundation, a continuation of the foundation that encouraged the publication of the collected work, organizes a yearly study day (or multiday conference), which focuses on a particular facet of Noordmans's work, always in the context of current thought. The lectures are published in separate booklets.

In the chapters that follow, the various phases of Noordmans's life are discussed, and, in that context, the development of his theology and his involvement in the course taken by the church are considered. Also noted is how his theology increasingly takes on the character of a theology of the Spirit. Many citations from Noordmans will be discussed in the text. At each place, the source will be noted. These citations are the central texts for the study of Noordmans, fragments which may give the flavor of his own peculiar way of thinking and writing.

CHAPTER 2

Youth and Education

Noordmans's Father and the Influence of the Réveil

Oepke Noordmans was born July 18, 1871, in Oosterend, Friesland, to a family active in church life. Following the death of his first wife, Oepke's father, Durk Piers Noordmans, married Gerbrig Oepkes de Roos. Oepke was the first child born to that marriage. His father was a farmer who was deeply interested in theology. He belonged to circles influenced by the Réveil, a movement that combined orthodox faith with a warm piety and that worked for a revival in the life of the church. He read the leaders of the Réveil with particular interest, such men as Isaäc da Costa, G. Groen van Prinsterer, J. A. Wormser, and W. de Clercq.

The Réveil was the continuation of seventeenth- and eighteenth-century pietism as it evolved in the nineteenth century. Modernism had arrived, and followers of the Réveil saw themselves as a counterforce to the new liberalism. In its original form, the Réveil tended toward world avoidance and the formation of covenanticles. But followers had become more aware of the objective validity of the gospel and of their shared responsibility for the entire church.

That was the case for Durk Piers Noordmans as well. In 1879 the family moved to Scharnegoutum, and there the senior Noordmans served for many years as an elder. He was a prominent member of the church council and for a period of time a member of the provincial synod's administrative body. Despite his deep concern for the condition of the Netherlands Reformed Church and his sympathy with those who advocated a greater authority for the church's confession, he was an opponent of the Doleantie, the movement led by Abraham Kuyper that, as a consequence of its faithfulness to the confessions, encouraged a division in the church. He was averse to division within the church; one must not desire the ruin of the church as an organization. Hence he considered himself an adherent to Ph. J. Hoedermaker (later the leader of the Confessional Party), with whom he corresponded. It was typical of his point of view that he removed his son Oepke from the Christian gymnasium[1] when the rector, the Reverend F.Ph.L.C. van Lingen, disclosed that he had joined the Doleantie.

For a number of years, the elder Noordmans was also a member of the municipal council of Wymbritseradeel, to which Scharnegoutum belonged. He represented the "Christian-Historicals," adherents of the idea of the re-Christianization of the nation. He was also an alderman within the same body for a number of years.

As a lay theologian he published a small pamphlet on baptism. In it he emphasized the objective validity of baptism, characterizing it as "an inexpressible, glorious exchange of state." The baptized are bearers of the "sign and seal of the covenant" and remain so, even when they are adherents of modernist or liberal ideas. In those cases, the congregation must recognize that it has been lax in its oversight and so bears the responsibility for the spreading of such ideas. It cannot simply reject its liberal members and so "throw them back into paganism."

Parental Home: Gymnasium

Oepke grew up in that environment. For his entire life he remained thankful for what he had received there. When he accepted his honorary doctorate in Groningen, in 1935, he spoke of the "womb of piety in which my theology is embedded." By that he referred to the "church as mother" more than as an institution, to the church as a "home" church. It was the place "where scripture was read *viva voce*," where the "mystic tones of the psalms and hymns" echoed, and prayer was not a formulary but was "modulated as the Spirit gave expression."

---

[1]   [Trans. The American equivalent is high school. "High school" in Dutch refers to something more like an American junior college.]

In his later meditations he returns repeatedly to the environment of his upbringing. He does so in the meditation, "These Three," on 1 Corinthians 13:13. Faith, hope, and love, identified in this text as those which "abide," remind him of the three long and wide oaken pipes—a, b sharp, and b—as a "bonus from the organ builder" in the organ in the home of his youth. They were pipes that were not part of the usual house organ, yet they could "just stand" and "gave a solid foundation to the playing of the music." That is the case with faith, hope, and love: they "are nearly too large and too powerful to have a place in the instrument of life, in the space in which they exist." Noordmans reworks something of the memories of his youth around these three organ pipes.

> When on a quiet evening, at the hour when the evening-psalm was sung, I came home from elsewhere, these three voices echoed in my ear when I was still a half-mile away. I was admitted from afar into this cathedral of sound....No cathedral organ has ever been able to give me a feeling of consecration as *these three*, when they erected a temple around the dwelling. And no church ever gave me such certainty of coming home to God.[2]

Thus it was all the more painful for him when the harmonic unity of that home church was ruined by the Doleantie. "The division of 1886 went directly through the family to which I belonged. Half went with what was then called the Doleantie; the other half didn't." He uttered that sentence in a lecture held in 1935 at the Vrije Universiteit,[3] in which he did not hide his joy over the invitation to offer the lecture in that location: "I have the feeling as though this evening I see the other half of the larger family, that broke in two in 1886, before me."

In 1886 Oepke had already left home. The previous year, he had begun his education in the gymnasium. The principal of Oepke's first elementary school, the Christian School in Oosterend, had made it clear to his father, with whom he was a good friend, that it would be well not to have Oepke follow in his father's profession as a farmer, but rather to have him study. So Oepke left in 1885 for Zetten and there became a student in the Christian gymnasium, the first of its kind in the Netherlands. One of his teachers there later called him one of the best students, "A young man with much talent, a good will and a sound mind." For many of the students, education in the gymnasium meant

---

[2]   *Verzamelde Werken* (Kampen: Kok, 1978-2004), 8:387f. Hereinafter *VW*, followed by the volume and page.

[3]   [Trans. Free University]

preparation for theological study. I already noted that the rector (and founder) of the school, the Reverend Van Lingen, represented himself ever more clearly as an advocate of the Doleantie—which penetrated the atmosphere of the school. That, in the long run, was the reason Oepke's father withdrew him from the gymnasium in Zetten. His further education took place in the city gymnasium in Sneek. There he received his diploma in 1891.

Theological Studies: Leiden and Utrecht

Noordmans began his theological studies that same year in Leiden. He broke them off after a year to continue in Utrecht. While in Leiden he was attracted to J. H. Gunning Jr., a professor of the philosophy of religion and earlier professor of dogmatics and Dutch church history in Amsterdam. Gunning was one of the founders of the Ethical Party in the church, a tradition inspired by the Réveil that emphasized that "truth" is concerned not only with thought but also touches heart and life. (The word *ethical* is derived from *ethos*, inward existence, mind.) This tradition would have a great influence on the development of Noordmans's thinking.

Noordmans himself later expressed deep gratitude for the contact he had with Gunning. He did so in a short contribution to a collection of essays in honor of Gunning, published in 1929 on the occasion of Gunning's one hundredth birthday. Noordmans writes, "To have known Gunning is a privilege...the impression has remained, my entire life." He considered Gunning's lectures as "lessons which were at the same time gospel preaching."

Nevertheless, from the outset Noordmans was not without criticism of Gunning. He must have expressed something of that in a letter to his father (subsequently lost), who also had reservations concerning ethical theology, which he viewed as dangerously tempting. Durk Noordmans missed in Gunning a clear choice between modernism and science on the one side and an orthodoxy faithful to scripture on the other. He feared that, with Gunning, matters would ultimately end up in modernism.

In a letter dated October 2, 1891, the elder Noordmans wrote this warning to his son: "Of the two one: either to the law and the witnesses or to science. One may now prattle of the inspiration of the Spirit in the hearts of believers, but if Holy Scripture has no decisive authority, then finally the spirit of the human himself will be the judge between this so-called inspiration and the fantasies of one's own notorious human heart." It must have been heartening to him that his son apparently was not prepared to allow himself to be drawn into the "stream" of Gunning's "tempting system." Oepke's original reservations, however, were quickly overcome by wonderment for what he received in his meeting with Gunning. And yet, he did not allow himself to be drawn in fully and would later have reservations of another sort about ethical theology.

During this same time Gunning's son, J.H. Gunning J.H.zn., was a preacher in Leiden. Erudite and irenic, with an inclination to evangelization, he shared his father's love for the church. He had great ecumenical interests and called himself "evangelical-catholic." He was a pastor to students and was available to help them in their studies, as, for example, in the Hebrew language. The young Noordmans made his acquaintance, and this connection also remained for his entire life. He took his catechetical education from the young Gunning and, on Easter 1892, made public confession of faith under his guidance.

During that one year of study in Leiden, Noordmans witnessed that the other professors were active primarily as representatives of the Modernist Party[4] in the church. For example, in biblical studies and in the science of religion they pursued a theology that was, to Noordmans's thinking, far from the concrete congregation. He would later describe this as the sharp contrast between "school" and "church."

As stated above, Noordmans continued his studies in Utrecht in 1892. There it was primarily the professor of Old Testament, J. J. P. Valeton Jr., a leader of the younger ethicals, who made an impression on him. Valeton connected historical-critical biblical studies with Christian faith; that earned for him the reproach of half-heartedness from the modernist side—a well-known reproach laid to the ethicals from both modernists and orthodox. As for the rest, Noordmans came across professors in Utrecht who were more scholarly than spiritual. And he came into contact with his former pastor from Leiden, the young Gunning, who had become a minister in Utrecht in 1894.

Illness and Delay

During this time Noordmans struggled with a serious illness. He must have suffered from over-exertion. In any case, the illness caused

---

4   [Trans. Dutch *richting*. This term, literally "direction," is used of groups of differing theological inclinations within the church. The Dutch church would later use the term "modality," or a way of being in the church, to describe the *richtingen*. However, the groups were often very organized, with membership, leadership, publications, etc., and this translation uses the term "party," analogous to a political party.]

him to interrupt his studies for a few years, beginning in 1893. He also stayed for some time at a health resort in Switzerland. But in 1898 he was back in Utrecht, still under medical care. He had plans to take a doctoral exam (not yet required for ministerial education), but they were not to be realized. On May 29, 1902, he passed his ecclesiastical examination. Two weeks later he preached his test sermon. On September 10 of the same year he was admitted to the ministry of the gospel. And on February 1, 1903, he was installed in the office of preacher in his first congregation, Idsegahuizen and Piaam.

The considerable delay in the completion of his ministerial education had a significant influence on Noordmans's formation. In one of his later meditations one can hear echoes of that experience. The meditation is on the call of Moses (Exod. 4:12). As the Bible story tells it, Moses could not simply appear as a liberator of his people. His first attempt in this direction stumbled over resistance from his own people. He had to flee and continue elsewhere before he was called by God to lead his people out of Egypt. At this point he hesitates.

So quick to anger and so prepared to act as he was at the end of the first period of his life, so difficult is it for him to accept the task of leading Israel out of Egypt as it is laid on him...Moses had learned that it is not sufficient when blood speaks...Now comes God, now comes the Spirit to teach him to speak.[5]

In the course of Moses' life, says Noordmans, a *retardatie*, (i.e., delay) appeared. That delay has made Moses into a new man. The first Moses has become a second. "It is an awesome thing when the Spirit takes creation *once again* in hand." Where that happens, life is given its real meaning. In this context, Noordmans is speaking of the Christian life. "A Christian is someone who has noticed that one cannot simply live straight-forward. The Spirit is a principle of regression, of *retardatie*, of delay." That happens to be true, says Noordmans, also in a biological sense, for human life as such. In comparison with animal life, it "comes the farthest because it has been delayed the most. That is the case in the full sense of the life from the Spirit...Life is given not once, but twice."

It is highly improbable that Noordmans, in writing this meditation, was not also thinking of the course of his own life, of the delay that he had to suffer on account of his own illness.

[5]   *VW* 8:194.

CHAPTER 3

First Years in Ministry

Idsegahuizen and Piaam

Oepke Noordmans was installed as preacher in his first congregation in Idsegahuizen and Piaam February 1, 1903. As a bachelor, but under the care of a housekeeper, he lived in the parsonage in Idsegahuizen. Both tiny villages (together not more than three hundred inhabitants) lie on the coast of the Ysselmeer (then the Zuiderzee), in the west of Friesland. At the time it was a very desolate area. Each village had a church building. Noordmans had to lead services every Sunday in both churches, one in the morning and the other in the afternoon, the villages taking turns with the service times.

The Doleantie had influenced this area as well. A small group of members had separated from the local Reformed church and had constituted itself as a *Gereformeerde*[1] church. In a letter to the church

---

1   [Trans. The terms *gereformeerde* and *hervormde* present a problem in English. Both terms mean "reformed." When referring to a particular denomination, the Netherlands Reformed Church, the term *hervormde* is used. When referring to the denomination formed by the events of 1834 and 1886—when churches left the

11

council of Reformed Idsegahuizen-Piaam, this group had introduced itself as the legitimate representative of the local *Gereformeerde* (i.e., "truly Reformed") church and demanded from the Reformed church council the transfer of baptismal records, membership books, and diaconal possessions. The Reformed church council had not conceded. Such were the relations only fifteen years prior to Noordmans's arrival.

Meanwhile, in Piaam, a separate *Gereformeerde* church was built right next to the Reformed church's building. Organizationally, the *Gereformeerde* congregations in Idsegahuizen and Piaam had combined with the *Gereformeerden* of two neighboring villages, Gaast and Ferwoude. A brother-in-law of Noordmans, who was married to his half-sister Anna (from his father's first marriage), was the minister of this united *Gereformeerde* church. The two brothers-in-law were thus active in the same area. Matters would become even more complex when Noordmans later became a consultant to the Reformed congregation in Gaast-Ferwoude. The family relationships were not without tension, certainly when it came to church matters. Because Anna's bridegroom was *Gereformeerd,* her father was not present at the church blessing of his daughter's marriage, although he attended the civil ceremony. The situation illustrates how painfully sharp the relationships between Reformed and *Gereformeerd* were at that time. Those feelings must have had their effect on the relationships within Noordmans's greater family.

Opening Sermon

Noordmans's first sermon in Idsegahuizen had as its text Matthew 13:3-9, the parable of the sower. Different kinds of soil are sketched in the parable. They indicate different types of hearers, according to the interpretation appended within the gospel itself. The seed is the image of the preached Word. The seed is good; it is the same sower who sows the seed. Still, as a consequence of the difference in soil, the seed does not bear fruit everywhere. According to the parable only part of the seed falls on good earth. It is the earth that brings forth good fruit.

The parable gave Noordmans the occasion to reflect on the relationship between the Word and the human heart. Where the Word falls on good earth, there is, he said, a "relationship between the word and the heart." There is

a convergence, an agreement, so that the powers of the word make the heart alive and likewise the word becomes living as it

broader national body—the term *gereformeerde* is used. For that reason, the term will be left untranslated in the text, while "Reformed" refers to the older church body.]

is received in the heart. For what is the seed if it does not fall in a field? And put the other way, what is the field if it is not sown? It is just through this unity of word and heart that the fruit must be seen. The fruits are then not independent, something additional, but they are born out of the word and out of the heart, out of the union of the two. If there was no word, i.e., no divine, life-giving love, the heart would become and remain a cold and despairing soil of all evil. But it is also so that if there was no heart that needed love, that was thirsty for it, the love would not be felt and could not kindle mutual love. So out of the union of word and the heart that longs for salvation the most beautiful fruit is born.[2]

The Ethical Party

Already in this opening sermon, Noordmans strikes a tone that we will also hear in his later work. We can call it the *ethical* tone. It concerns what Noordmans elsewhere calls "the humane character of Christian truth," a description that was characteristic of the Ethical Party in the Reformed Church. We have already met that stream of thought in the previous chapter. Noordmans's teacher Gunning was one of its founders. Toward the end of his life, Noordmans offered a short description of the Ethical Party. It derived its name, he said, from its emphasis that "truth is *ethical*." That means that truth is not simply identical with "what is stated in the Bible or what the confessions say," nor with "what experience or thought offer." No,

> every thought, every act must, if one would draw a conclusion from it or reach a goal with it, first go through the heart. Otherwise the conclusion is too hard, the goal too loveless. When this passage through the heart into life takes place more and more, then the human does not remain unchanged. Ethical theology was a theology of regeneration. It stood against all that is "brave" and "bold" in thought and action that knows nothing of the broken heart nor takes it into account.[3]

Noordmans speaks here in the past tense. When he wrote this in 1952 the ethical tradition no longer really existed in the church, as he himself noted. The word *ethical* "is, as an appellation of an ecclesiastical party, now out of date." And, as he added ironically, "There are for the

2   *VW* 1:23f.
3   *VW* 3:503f.

people of the church some advantages connected with that. For it was difficult for most people to form a clear image of what 'ethical' really meant."

At the time the overriding contrast in the Reformed Church was between the "confessionals" and the "modernists" ("liberals"). The confessionals fought for official recognition in the church of the authority of the confessional writings including, where necessary, doctrinal discipline. In their opinion, that was the only way the church could be restored. The modernists (liberals), on the other hand, would have nothing to do with maintaining the confessions. They fought for a church in which freedom of doctrine was allowed and which would have a place for new and modern insights of faith. The battle between the parties was heavy, even following the events of the Doleantie.

The ethicals did not find themselves represented in this opposition between confessionals and modernists. They were not modernists, but they did not allow themselves to be enlisted on the confessional front either. Faith, in their view, the truth of faith, was too much an existential matter to allow that. They were averse to the formal maintenance of confession as well as to juridical discipline. Such means did not serve faith understood as a lived truth. Truth itself must be able to work in human hearts. Juridical discipline can only harm truth. Discipline, where necessary, must be "medical," able to assist the healing powers of the body of the church itself. Its goal must be not to cut the ill out but to save them. That could bring about not so much the possibility of the *restoration* of the church but of church *renewal*. The aim would not be a return to the past but openness to the future.

These ideas did not fit well with the ecclesiastical discussions of the time. Neither the confessional nor the liberal side knew what to make of the ethicals. They refused to be enrolled in either party. Their ideas did not lend themselves to popular propaganda. They never had a large following. In the reflection cited above Noordmans wrote, "The Ethical Party consisted only of officers; it had no soldiers."

Among the confessionals in particular there existed little sympathy for ethical theology. They deemed its ideas too vague, insufficiently concrete. We have already seen that Noordmans's father had his reservations about ethical theology as represented by Gunning, his son's teacher. Noordmans originally shared these reservations, but for him they were soon overcome by feelings of respect and gratitude. He would feel most at home with the ethicals.

Even while he was student, Noordmans's sympathy for ethical theology had evoked strong criticism, even within his own family.

It emerged when Noordmans preached his test sermon at the end of his ministerial education, on June 12, 1902. His parents were not present; to have been present at that moment would, they feared, have been too much for them. However, other family members were present. One of them, a nephew, himself a confessional preacher, wrote Noordmans an extremely critical letter the following day. According to this correspondent, Noordmans had not only failed to follow the confessional point of view, but he had even "steamed past the ethical critical station." Noordmans had given a "purely modernist" sermon, far from "the glorious gospel of grace and salvation." The letter writer had, as he put it, little faith in Noordmans's future in the church. He would repeat this criticism in later letters. Noordmans's first sermon in Idsegahuizen was certainly not one to have changed his mind.

Others, however, noted Noordmans's relationship with ethical theology with respect and esteem. A colleague and contemporary, a preacher in the neighboring village of Makkum, looked back on Noordmans's years in Idsegahuizen and Piaam in a letter written years later: "By virtue of your upbringing you could have been an exceptional confessional preacher, you have been saved from that danger." Noordmans had, he wrote further, learned "to listen to other voices than that of the three formulae" (i.e., the three classic Reformed confessional writings, often designated as the "three formulae of unity").

"The humane character of Christian truth"

Noordmans had a great deal of work to do in his small congregation. In 1908 he also became a substitute (deputy preacher) of the congregation in the neighboring community of Gaast-Ferwoude (the same place where his brother-in-law was preacher of the *Gereformeerde* church), which had become vacant. Home visitation and visitation of the sick required a great deal of time. Noordmans traveled by bicycle, bus, and boat, but he still found time for further study. Soon, people came from ever wider distances to call on his abilities. In this way he became active in gatherings in the "ring Makkum" (the regional ministerial gathering). He was active organizationally—he took on a number of administrative duties—and even more so theologically. He was happy to participate in substantive discussions on papers by his ministerial colleagues, and he quickly became known for his theological (and philosophical) competence. He lectured a number of times for the ring Makkum.

He also became a member—later part of the board—of the Friesian Preachers Union, a society that had been recently established for "orthodox preachers" in Friesland (apparently Noordmans was considered orthodox). He continued to offer his theological input to this group, even after he had left his first congregation. The Friesian Preachers Union had published a paper since 1907, the *Reformed Sunday Paper for the Province of Friesland*. For a time, Noordmans was a member of the editorial board. He published many articles and series in that periodical, mostly between 1911 and 1915, on current church questions, articles that sometimes were the occasion for much discussion. A number of times he also lectured for this society. The first time was in Leeuwarden in 1906. He spoke on the subject, "Dogmatic Certainty." This lecture offers a striking example of how Noordmans's ethical thinking developed.

In this lecture we come across the expression already cited, "the humane character of Christian truth." Noordmans argues that that notion was already in mind during the Reformation and that it differed as much from the churches of Eastern Orthodoxy as it did from the Roman Catholic Church. In Eastern Orthodox dogmas, the great classic truths of the faith were "incorporated as holy formulae in the cult." There they stood outside of life, as objects of worship, "holy relics." In the Roman Catholic Church, dogmas were made safe via the infallible doctrinal authority of the church. That also kept them outside of life. Human belief there meant belief in the authority of the church, and only as such, by implication, assent to the truths of belief itself. But for Protestants faith, substantive faith, had become a personal matter. And unlike the Roman Catholic Church of the Middle Ages, the Reformation answered the question of the possibility of the certainty of salvation with an unconditional yes.

> If we may use an image, we would say: the man of the Middle Ages experiences himself as in an ark on the waters. Above is the starry heaven of revealed knowledge of God. The revealed truths are given. He may group them as one puts stars together into constellations. That is the exciting work of scholasticism with its awesome systems. And beneath him are the waves of mysticism, into which he can dive. Above the firmament, beneath an element. Both impersonal....With the Reformation it is as if God said another time: "Let us make men." The relations become smaller, but sharper, more spiritual, more personal.[4]

Here belief as knowledge (as "certain knowing") and as confidence come together in the human heart. The Reformation had taken a step from

4   *VW* 1:56f.

which there was no retreat. It is true, however, that later on problems and difficulties arose.

It is, Noordmans said, primarily the German theologian Friedrich Schleiermacher who is to be thanked for calling a halt within Protestantism in the nineteenth century to what had become a dominant, one-sided intellectualism. One could again appreciate the collation of belief and believing consciousness. Thus a fundamental insight of the Reformation reemerged and was increasingly emphasized, as in the ethical theology of the Netherlands. Faith, the content of faith, touches the heart. In that sense it is rightly said, "Christian truth has a humane character."

The Reformation did not intend to deny or to attack Christian, early church, dogmas; it was not about a "reduction of Christian thought," as would be the case with modernism. But its manner of dealing with dogma was different from that of Roman Catholicism or Eastern Orthodoxy. Here, "the need of the heart has worked eclectically in the reception of dogmata." Some truths simply appeared less important than others, for they didn't touch the heart as deeply and thus moved to the background. Noordmans identifies Schleiermacher as the one who had taken this principle with greater seriousness *vis à vis* the inclination, which had in the meantime emerged in Protestantism, to emphasize the objective character of belief, for example by appealing to external authority:

> Christian truth is here viewed from the perspective of consciousness. All care is taken here that it does not hover above the human, but rests in his heart....Here, principally, methodically, the Reformed principle "the one on behalf of the other" is taken seriously. Here dogma becomes much more dependent on the moral.[5]

Noordmans agrees: what is decisive for that which belongs in Christian dogmatics is the question "of the possibility of moral appropriation." Whoever allows the truths of belief to stand as objective truths in themselves makes of them, as it were, an algebra. Dogmatics, then, all too quickly becomes "a flat kind of logic." The matter itself then has been strained.

> When we advocate the humane character of Christian truth, that is not in contradiction to the divine character, but then we

---

[5]　*VW* 1:60f.

resist the sub-human, the purely intellectual, the rationalistic conception.[6]

That is what it is about. When we "descend into the life of faith" with our truths of faith, they become "clothed in flesh and muscles."

It is true, we must be alert to the misunderstanding that would view Christian consciousness not only as "the nature of truth" but as the "measure of truth" as well. In Noordmans's opinion, this misunderstanding was not completely absent from the Ethical Movement. He emphasized that Christian truth is not only about serving the "practice of life" but also a "theoretical view of life." There are not only "Christian states of mind" but also "the realities of the kingdom of God"—what Noordmans would call the "metaphysical point"—with which they are "connected." Christian truth is assuredly "for the human" but not "according to the human," let alone "from the human."

This is how Noordmans transcends the objective-subjective dilemma. When Peter confesses, "You are the Messiah, the Son of the living God" (Matt. 16:16), that is a metaphysical expression that far exceeds his understanding. Still, it is in line with the other confession we have received from Peter, spoken from his experience: "Lord, to whom can we go? You have the words of eternal life" (John 6:68). His first confession is included in the last. Peter's consciousness "points to it as the compass does to the North Pole."

His identification of the misunderstanding of subjectivism does not weaken Noordmans's query concerning the humane character of Christian truth. "We have the right to ask that dogma apply to our conscience." That is a request that, in his opinion, the theology of Abraham Kuyper and his neo-Calvinist followers overlooks. Noordmans characterizes that theology, typified by its attempt to derive everything from the Bible, as "scholastic" and "conceptual work," and, strikingly, as "cool and thin":

> I have a great deal of admiration for the systematic work of neo-Calvinist theologians. But I am of the opinion that they are cocooning themselves in a scholasticism that does not support the Christian life of the twentieth century, as one expects from it. As we reject scholasticism, we also reject erecting constructions from the letter of scripture.... Just so we do not overcome the situation of the Greeks and the Catholics, but again, essentially,

6   *VW* 1:63.

arrive at one dogma! The Catholics—the church. The Protestants—scripture....All dogmas...must obtain their certainty from a detour by way of scripture. There is then no immediate contact....To put it simply, this means that something is true because it is in the Bible, just as the Catholic accepts something because the church says it....If the Roman Catholic Church has robbed dogma of its power by canonizing it, I think that danger lies along this same way in that dogma is robbed of its power through "scripturizing" it. When it is demanded that one stand in the same relationship of faith to Jonah and the whale as one does to the resurrected Christ—both on the ground of external authority—then this must result in the negation of the moral force of truth and ultimately of the authority of scripture itself.[7]

In contradistinction Noordmans holds that what is at stake is not truth in itself but that it is given "judging and liberating power." In that way, we come to dogmatic certainty.

The Historic Character of Christian Truth

In 1909, it was again Noordmans's turn to present a lecture at the Friesian Preachers Union. This time, his subject was, "The Witness of De Hartog." Dr. A. H. de Hartog, Reformed minister and later professor, the father of the author Jan de Hartog, had been a classmate of Noordmans in Utrecht, and their relationship would remain friendly even into their later years. De Hartog was a passionate defender of the faith as well as a polemicist who wished to engage in debate with both modernists and orthodox. It was particularly from those on the right, however, that he had to endure a sharp critique. It was this criticism that motivated Noordmans to make De Hartog's ideas the subject of his reflections. "The fury with which one, in an old-national manner, has opened fire on Dr. de Hartog" touched him personally. De Hartog was present at the gathering where Noordmans gave his lecture. In the discussion that followed, he offered an extensive response to Noordmans's argument. Later, Noordmans reworked his lecture into an article for the journal, *Stemmen voor Waarheid en Vrede* [Voices for truth and peace], a paper that represented ethical theology. The article appeared in 1910 and was Noordmans's first publication.

De Hartog did not intend his reflections on faith to remain with the "facts of salvation" of 1900 years past (as is the habit of orthodox

---

[7] *VW* 1:72.

believers). For him the point at stake was what was behind the facts, and so behind the appearance of Jesus: the "great decree of God," God's own power and wisdom. He did not want to see the gospel reduced to a notarial act concerning there and then; rather, he understood it, while referring to what has happened, essentially as "the Word of God that *remains* to eternity." According to De Hartog, then, the point is not about the cross on Golgotha but the "eternal cross in God's creation," of which the historical cross was a representation; not the Christ himself as described in the gospels, but the "cosmic Christ" in the background.

Noordmans begins by supporting De Hartog. He experiences De Hartog's enthusiastic attempt to make Christian truth understandable, "evident to both heart and head," as beneficial, particularly in comparison with an orthodoxy that appeals formally to scripture and no further. But then he offers a word of "brotherly criticism." God's revelation in history, as the Bible narrates it, is not given to us in order that we seek or construct the real matter through it or behind it. No, we must remain with history, revelation, itself. It means to address us as "word." Revelation is the means through which we are able to learn to know God. We remain bound to that means. We cannot bypass it. In faith we have to stick to that means (we can do no other). Thus we do not arrive at the "impenetrable eternal Essence" (as De Hartog prefers to call God) but meet "the Father of our Lord Jesus Christ." De Hartog may be primarily interested in the "cosmic Christ," but that, in Noordmans's argument, is a profundity that provokes more fear than it does comfort.

> The "Eternal" in Dr. De Hartog's writings is someone other for us than the Father of whom no one comes except through the Son. And the cosmic Christ who appears out of the depths of reality reminds us more of the spirit which Faust feared than of the Son, full of grace and truth.[8]

We can thus better avoid profound speculations and remain with the biblical proclamation of the Human Christ Jesus, the one Mediator of God and the human.

Just as we saw Noordmans advocate for the "humane character of Christian truth" in his lecture, "Dogmatic Certainty," we see him here, in a continuation of that argument, advocating its historic character. However, that is not to say that belief would cherish antiquities! It is just his objection to current orthodoxy that it fixates on the "historicity"

---

[8]   *VW* 1:165.

of the facts of salvation in themselves, as one would view pictures in books about the past. In that criticism he stands with De Hartog. But he emphasizes, differently from De Hartog, history as it meets us, as events that have their impact on us. He had already done that in his lecture, "Dogmatic Certainty." There he had not only erected a front against orthodoxy, but also against modernism. "Rationalism that intends to fabricate truth from the naked intellect knows no greater enemy than history."

So Noordmans arrived at a sharp rejection of the content of De Hartog's theological ideas. This did not lead to a break in their friendship. De Hartog could accept Noordmans's criticism and even respect it. He thought, though, that Noordmans misunderstood him. It is more important for us to see how Noordmans, already in his first publication, struck a tone that we will later hear from him in a stronger form: belief is bound to the authority of revelation.

CHAPTER 4

Years of Conflict

Suameer

In 1910 Oepke Noordmans received and accepted a call to the congregation in Suameer, located in the Friesian Forest in the southeast corner of Friesland. It had been a poor area from time immemorial. In 1910, social conditions began to improve. Some industry began to appear. In Noordmans's years there a train line began service and drew Suameer from its isolation.

The majority of the population consisted of members of the Reformed Church. Pietism—a movement that emphasized the experience of the faith—had left its imprint in the eighteenth century. It had led to separate worship services. But there was little inclination to separate officially from the church. In any case the Doleantie had found little foothold in Suameer and its environs.

The congregation of about one thousand (out of a total population of about thirteen hundred) was larger than the one in Idsegahuizen and Piaam. There was not only a difference in size. During his time in Suameer, Noordmans would experience a number of different kinds of tension and conflict. These conflicts would have consequences for both his thought and his ecclesiastical life.

Beginning of a New Stage of Life

Seen from another point of view, 1910 was the onset of a new stage in his life. Two years earlier, Noordmans had made the acquaintance of Johanna Hillegonda ("Jo") Oosterhuis, daughter of the minister at Suawoude and Tietjerk. She was born in 1886, and so fifteen years younger than Noordmans, and she lived with her brother, also a minister in Friesland. Their acquaintance had pleased them both, and in December 1909 they had become engaged. At the beginning of Noordmans's ministry in Suameer, he was installed by his soon-to-be father-in-law. Four days later the pair was married.

One of Noordmans's colleagues put into words what this change meant for him: "Lonely vagabond, sitting down to a cold hearth in a silent house, near the cold and salty dampness of the sea, consulting dry philosophers and fruitlessly seeking warmth with those who are sharp of spirit and are not able to cherish the heart and now—to the mild forest with Jo! That says it all." G. J. Paul, who was the first to publish a dissertation on Noordmans in 1959, writes concerning Noordmans's wife, "With her God gave him the great happiness of a richly blessed marriage and a close and tender family life. It is not possible to conceive of Noordmans's theological and ecclesiastical work without the power and the rest which came from this 'home church' and extended for all of his life."

His parents did not witness this double "new beginning." His father had already died in 1907. His mother still lived and could have known of his engagement. In April 1910, Noordmans could send her the report of the call he had received and accepted. But she died on May 16 of that year, nearly two months before he began in Suameer.

A daughter, Rutgerdina Adelpha, was born to that marriage in 1912. In 1915 a son, Dirk Petrus (who would die at the end of the occupation of the Second World War), arrived, and in 1923 a second son, Johannes Arnoldus.

Wide View

As minister in Suameer, Noordmans remained active in provincial and regional affairs. Thus, he continued his work in the Friesian Preachers Union. In his later years at Suameer, he offered courses in the Dokkum section of the Peoples' University.[1] The subjects he taught there

---

[1] [Trans. Not a university in the proper sense but an organization for general education in a number of subjects, with courses offered throughout the nation.]

give us a sense of his interest in the relationship between Christendom and culture. Both ancient and modern thinkers (Cicero and Descartes, for example) were on the agenda, as were important figures from church history (Augustine, Luther, Schleiermacher). Noordmans would continue on this track in later years. Another way he was active in the broader context was with the Friesian union Kinderzorg [child care]. The diaconates in Friesland had established this union (as they had in other provinces and regions) to fulfill together what had been formulated in 1906 as a new ecclesiastical regulation for deacons: the care and education of orphans belonging to the church and of children in need of help. Noordmans became secretary of Kinderzorg in 1910. In this capacity, he provided yearly reports, which were published as appendixes of the *Hervormd Zondagsblad*. Still, his primary accent was on his activities in Suameer.

A meditation on Matthew 2:1-12, the story of the Wise Men who came from the East to worship the baby Jesus, dates from this period, 1912. Later (in 1946) Noordmans published it in a collection with other, later meditations. In it one can hear clearly something of how his preaching sounded in Suameer. Noordmans speaks of the puzzle that these Wise Men represent within the context of the entire gospel. They "became as visible as meteors only to disappear without a trace. They are...representatives of the unknown millions who want nonetheless to be represented at the crib of the Lord." And then he places the gospel over and against a narrow ecclesiastical mentality.

> We readily calculate. From the dwellers of the earth we first subtract the pagans. Next the Jews and Mohammedans. We keep the Christians. But we go further. Greek Catholics and Roman Catholics are out of our view. We keep the Protestants. Many branches of Protestantism are strange to us. *Our spiritual family is small*....There the Wise Men from the East stand beside the crib. They come by way of Jerusalem. But the scribes will certainly have had no time to make them proselytes first. They wouldn't want to....Uncatechized they come to the light...God has some direct methods which are not our own....God's family is large.[2]

Obstinence

Noordmans did not have it easy in Suameer, where he would remain until 1923. His troubles had a good deal to do with his own

---

[2]   *VW* 8:61.

disposition. He seemed odd to many folk. His sermons (here again he had to preach every Sunday at both the morning and afternoon services) were soon judged too difficult. People stayed away from church simply because they could not understand him, but also because they were dissatisfied with what they had understood all too well. Others were attracted by his sermons; you could learn from him.

In any case, Noordmans did not play up to people. He let that be known already in his opening sermon in Suameer. He said, "We hope that you will be satisfied with our preaching. However, we do not believe that it is good *always* to be satisfied with God's Word." He could be brusque when he did not agree on particular matters, even with certain ecclesiastical rules. That would sometimes bring him into conflict with the church council during the worship service. He didn't avoid the conflict. In his closing sermon he laid his cards on the table.

> The dominee must be everyone's friend: a Joris Goodblood. The peace pipe must smolder and burn uninterruptedly. But I ask you: is then the guy not alive? Does he not preach? Or was I... incorrigible? I wouldn't happily put it like that. But in the main, in the intentions of my feeling, honest to my word, I would do it again, and I call on God as witness, I could do no other.[3]

He was stiff in manner. Alongside his stiffness was the difficulty he had visiting the sick. He had a phobia of germs, and to avoid the danger of infection he kept himself as far as possible from the ill. During a sick visit, by way of precaution, he kept his gloves on. In some cases he used his handkerchief or a walking stick to open the door of the room or of the cupboard-bed. Behaviors like these betrayed his peculiarity.

As minister in Suameer, Noordmans was by definition president of the board of the local Christian school. From the outset he engaged enthusiastically in Christian education. After a few years, however, disagreements arose between Noordmans and the head of school. Noordmans stumbled over what he considered the headmaster's arbitrariness. In turn, the head of school thought himself attacked by the president. Mediation through the national organization, CVO (Christian Peoples Education), did not succeed. Finally, the direct connection between the church council and the school board ended by virtue of a change in the law. However, the relationship between the head of school and the minister remained tense—all the more so when the head of school was chosen to be an elder. Noordmans sent his own

---

3   *VW* 7:416-18.

children to public school. Ultimately these involvements had their effect on the life of the church. Churchgoing in Suameer dwindled.

Conflicts with the Church Wardens

The primary conflicts were with the church wardens,[4] charged as they were with the administration of the financial and material matters of the church. According to the regulations applicable at the time, the church wardens enjoyed a far-reaching autonomy within the congregation *vis à vis* the church council. In Suameer, problems originated because the church wardens refused to pay the costs of bread and wine for the celebration of the Lord's Supper. For a long time the diaconate paid those costs out of the money that was in fact intended for social support. That was forbidden by the classical administration. The danger arose that the celebration of the Supper could no longer be held, but ultimately the church wardens reversed course.

This was an issue that did not concern Noordmans personally. A different question arose, however, because for a few years the church wardens did not fulfill their financial duties in the payment of the minister (and in that they were supported by the church council). Noordmans did not let matters slide and introduced an official complaint with the provincial church board. It agreed with him, so the matter was settled. But later, in 1918, something similar happened. That time, a judge had to intervene to force unwilling members of the congregation to pay their required contribution toward the preacher's salary.

Tensions remained. The classical administration established a special commission in 1919 to investigate the situation in Suameer. The commission concluded that the difficulties were in part due to Noordmans's own character, with his inclination to sail directly through the sea, but that they were primarily caused by the people's attitude. On that subject, the commission reported that the people would gladly "seek out" and attempt to "pinch" someone they did not like. "There are a number of farmers in the congregation who threaten the minister's family with starvation." The commission also voiced its disapproval of the fact that in Suameer it had been made necessary for the minister personally to solicit from congregational members part of his own salary (salary that was legitimately promised to him when he

---

[4]   [Trans. In Dutch, *kerkvoogdij*—a species of elder whose task it was to administer the financial affairs of the local congregation. These office-bearers gathered in a *beheer*— translated here as "administration," in distinction from the *bestuur*—the work of the church council to direct the administrative affairs of the congregation.]

came to the church). "The church council should *never* have allowed this to happen."

Maintenance of the parsonage also brought Noordmans and his wife into conflict with the church wardens. A request for a number of repairs to be done was rejected, with an appeal to the low balance in the wardens' treasury. Rather than complaining about the bad condition of the parsonage, the church wardens suggested that the minister should appeal to the congregation for larger offerings. Committing to a large maintenance would come down to "managing someone else's money." Noordmans reacted sharply, especially to this last response. As with the timely payment of the salary, he said, the good upkeep of the parsonage is a minister's right. Someone who fails here is already guilty of "managing someone else's money." The church wardens must be willing to change course and take responsibility themselves for the collection of the contributions of church members.

Run-ins like this happened repeatedly. There was also a conflict in 1921 on the occasion of naming one of the church wardens as an elder. The fact that the person in question would not subject himself as warden to a regulation instituted that year by the synod concerning ministers' salaries and, moreover, had personally refused to pay his contribution to the minister's salary gave Noordmans (along with a church member) the occasion to introduce a complaint with the classical administration against naming this warden as an elder. The complaint was upheld, but the man in question, supported by a group of church members, appealed to the provincial board. That appeal, too, was rejected. In protest the two other elders resigned. Reformed Suameer sat temporarily without a church council. The tasks of the church council were taken over (according to regulations) by the classical administration until a new church council could function.

Relationship with the Covenant of Netherlands Preachers

Thus Noordmans stood in the midst of the turbulence of church life. That gave him much to think and write about. He was convinced that his run-ins with the church wardens had to do with more than purely business matters. Likewise, the Covenant of Netherlands Preachers, established in 1918, had to do with more than advocating the interests of ministers. Of course the Covenant advocated (and advocates) for such interests. But it did (and does) so from the notion that it is in the interest of the church (and the preachers themselves!) to keep an eye on the peculiar nature of the preacher's ministry. When that is in view, one may trust that the promotion of the material interests of ministers will also be in order. Both ministers and church are better off when the minister can be about the work of his office free and unencumbered.

Noordmans was a cofounder of the Covenant and, from 1921 to 1928, a member of its board. When asked whether he was prepared to join the board, he had agreed. "Certainly, presence at the gatherings will be time consuming and I have resigned from several administrative functions these last years, in order not to cut my time into little bits. However, I think the business of the Covenant so important and relevant that I will not withdraw from it." Before he joined the board, he had given a lecture for ministers in Meppel in which he had disclosed his agreement in principle with the work of the Covenant for the betterment of ministers' salaries. He had already published a number of times in the *Organ*, the monthly publication of the recently established Covenant. As a member of the board Noordmans would continue expressing himself on what interested him in "the present position of the minister" through articles in the *Organ* and in pieces sent in to the *Nieuwe Rotterdamsche Courant.*

"The Present Position of the Minister"

Noordmans called attention to the super-spiritual manner in which the church, both officially and unofficially, viewed the minister. He argued that certain "spiritual" demands were placed on the minister in the congregation as though he were nothing other than a "holy functionary," a distributor of sacramental goods, much like the priest in the Roman Catholic parish of old. He pointed out that this is a clerical way of thinking, even within the Reformed Church. He sharply attacked the fact that the minister was evaluated primarily in his technical-sacramental function, not only by the congregation but also by the supralocal administration. A preacher is a "good" preacher when he does faithfully what he "must" do, when he executes the "business of the office" where he is "installed." When all goes well there is satisfaction and the congregation "blossoms." But it can go differently.

> Suppose...that a minister really does his spiritual work conscientiously. He establishes not only that the righteous will do well and the godless badly...but he calls a sheep a sheep and a goat a goat and a wolf a wolf. He doesn't do this with infallible knowledge but according to his honorable human conviction, so that he also might be wrong. He does not always wait until the church council has expressed a judgment with a majority of votes but acts as particular, distinguishing matters, what is closer

to a spiritual distinction than one on the ground of the articles in the regulations. In a word, he behaves himself as a man and not as a functionary. He works with his heart and not only with the apparatus of his office. Then assuredly the official work will suffer.[5]

Next, the administrative bodies of the church move into action, for regulations must be maintained. The preacher must be called to order (the order of the "holy functionaries"). It is no wonder that in such a climate, and with this understanding of office, action on behalf of the betterment of salaries was viewed as inappropriate.

Naturally, Noordmans said, the dominee is expected to preach. He must be a "pulpiteer." But he is also to remain free of all strife, avoid all conflict, and please everyone at all costs. Every Sunday a full church; that's the nicest. Whoever lives up to that ideal must "remain free of politics," and "mention societal life only in exceptional moments." "He may involve himself in the moral life only as a secondary matter." The pulpiteer is the dominee who trades in beautiful sounding, edifying, empty phrases. His sermons are, as it were, "holy rites." As with the Roman Catholic pastor, the pulpiteer's place is outside reality, in a "spiritual" realm. That's what the administrative bodies of the church and the regulations want from a dominee. They are set in place for rest, not for action.

Noordmans recognized here an essentially unreformed (non-Calvinistic) aspect to the ministry. Calvin would certainly not have the church and its ministers outside of moral, societal, and political life. Raising such questions, he pointed out, was not the hobby of a particular ecclesiastical party. Suppose that a division arose in a church between socialist and "Reformed" preachers. "This would be a wonderful confusion. Where the 'Reformed' minister remains a pulpiteer and the social minister seeks a connection with society, then, in this picture, the latter would be the most Reformed."

Noordmans pled that the minister be liberated from his imprisonment to the super-spiritual. The minister must be able to take his place in the midst of society. He has to be allowed to do his work truthfully, guided by his Christian faith. In fact, Noordmans went on, the minister's position often depends on the presence of funds, "dead" money. As such the minister's position is a feudal possession. It is true that in some cases a wealth of funds can lead to a high salary. But

[5]   *VW* 5:28.

the minister who is established in that local congregation could also, by definition, be nothing other than the possession of the village, an ornament of the village, useless for ordinary, daily life.

This coheres with the division between the church council and the church wardens. We saw how Noordmans found himself confronted with that reality in Suameer. He did not fail to point out the disaster of this division. It made church wardens regents to whom the minister was arbitrarily handed over. This situation needed to come to an end. He saw the new regulation for minister's salaries, accepted by the synod in 1921, as a step in the right direction. With that regulation, the church council began to involve itself in the church wardens' terrain.

But a change in attitude among ministers would also be important, Noordmans argued. They were often caught up in the existing situation. They saw it as freedom—specifically in view of the wardens, the church council, and their colleagues—without noticing how much they (in their so-called "free profession") in fact were imprisoned and isolated. Ministers would have to learn to unite, to form mutual solidarity, in a spiritual working community. That requires organization. Hence the importance of the Covenant of Netherlands Preachers as an organization "which mobilizes us." A battle would have to be engaged.

Noordmans did not hesitate to appeal to ministers openly. "Whoever is outlawed has the right to act as a buccaneer." That was no plea for absolute freedom for ministers or for their right to take the law into their own hands. If necessary the minister must become a "buccaneer" *vis à vis* church regulations that handicap him in doing the genuine work of the church, that is to function spiritually (not "super-spiritually"). It can also happen in society that "formal law leads to immorality." Then the judge intervenes or the legislator or public opinion. "We break into a home where a man abuses his wife or children, thus acting against the law." So the formal law, the regulation, must not have the last word in the church. Beyond the existing formal law a new law must be taken hold of, a new order, to be proposed from the true, Christian, and moral task of the church.

In this way, Noordmans was an articulate spokesman for the Covenant of Netherlands Preachers. He was appropriately called the "great ideologue" of the Covenant. In 1928 he ended his membership on the board of the Covenant because of the pressure of work, as he put it. But he continued to advocate for the reorganization of the church, of which the improvement of ministers' salaries was only a first step.

CHAPTER 5

Around 1920: A Shift in Thought

Social Questions

That Noordmans did not have it easy in Suameer is clear from the previous chapter. Run-ins were also a consequence of his position on social issues. In and around Suameer there were deep divisions between rich farmers and poor farm laborers. Noordmans was not a man to leave such matters unremarked. At issue was an injustice that must be set right. In his opinion, it was a matter of listening or not listening to God's demand for justice. He did not shy away from allowing this concern to be heard in his pastoral work. J. D. Th. Wassenaar cites the Friesian church historian, J. J. Kalma, who offers an illustration. A rich farmer requested to be received as a member of the church. Noordmans refused to comply until the farmer would first pay his laborers a higher wage.

Noordmans's position on social matters also appeared in his sermons, for example in a sermon on Matthew 7:21-23, probably from the end of 1918. In the text, Jesus talks about those who say to him, "Lord, Lord." They pay him homage, they even drive out demons from the possessed, appealing to Jesus' name. Jesus does not reject their enthusiasm, but he says that it is not for that reason alone that they will enter the kingdom of heaven. What it comes down to, says Jesus, is whether they "act according to the will of my heavenly Father." Noordmans's sermon reflects on this. For Jesus, spiritual enthusiasm is spectacular, but only of the moment. It is a "hallelujah-Christianity." "In the last twenty-five years we have had too much of that Christianity." Without regular, daily obedience it is worth nothing. What does obedience include? The inclination to justice and righteousness. Church members are often deaf to just that call.

It is in that connection that Noordmans alludes to recent events: the threatened revolution by the SDAP (Socialist) leader, Troelstra, who among other things turned against the House of Orange. Christian organizations were active in mobilizing public opinion on a massive scale. The number of demonstrations from those loyal to the ruling party and the royal house took on enormous proportions and included church members. Noordmans says that his heart is heavy. This threatens to become a civil war. Must the church share in that movement? "Some find that to be genuine Christianity." And it is precisely such people who "are deaf to the preaching of societal justice."

> I think of our prayer and thanksgiving services for harvests, where we have sometimes seriously raised the issue of social righteousness. Farmers are so anxious about that, that nearly none of them are present any longer as we pray and give thanks for the harvest. Would we be headed in the right direction if the church took hold of the sword rather than serve justice? I dare to predict. When the church takes that direction rather than the way of social righteousness, that is the last gasp of hallelujah-Christianity and then it is done for good. It is our hearts' desire that God protect and defend our House of Orange. But no Orange...can replace justice. He serves the House of Orange best who seeks as passionately as possible to fill the chasm that runs through our poor folk.[1]

"Communion and Personhood"

One could think that this openness to social questions does not cohere with Noordmans's relationship with the Ethical Party in the church. Did not ethical theology direct all its thought to the humane,

---

[1]   *VW* 7:117f.

existential character of Christian truth? So above all one would expect an interest in the individual human in his or her religious personhood, the human for whom the gospel penetrates personal life. Such was indeed Noordmans's interest, but that does not conflict with his openness to social questions. Indeed, viewed rightly, they cohere.

Noordmans made his position clear in a lecture he held April 30, 1919, at the annual gathering of the Netherlands Reformed Ministers Union, a few months after the sermon cited above. His subject was "Communion and Personhood." The text from this lecture was later published in two installments in *Stemmen voor Waarheid en Vrede*, the same journal where nine years earlier he had published his article, "The Witness of De Hartog."

We are inclined, he said, to see human life lived within fixed connections given in nature: family, society, church, state. Hence we could be satisfied keeping ourselves to biblical guidelines. But we can no longer do that, certainly not in social matters. The ordered context in which everyone has his or her fixed place has begun to collapse. In the world of work, of economy, questions arise that cannot be answered simply by appealing to biblical texts. There it is the case that "Christian" includes more than "biblical." Still, social changes touch personal life. Precisely because the ordered contexts of the past, with fixed places for everyone, are breaking apart, everyone must learn to stand on his or her own feet. Now the issue at stake is to become a true "person." At the same time, we note that the same social developments press hard against human personhood. The threat grows that the human will be lost (or go under) in the community. "Humanity suffers." Socially, much can be done to improve the conditions of life.

> Improvement in wages, working conditions, a shorter workday, etc., all that creates space for personal life....But! Will there still be values and persons, bearers of value, to fill the constructed space? That is what the "socials" must ask themselves. The conditions, supposing they can be created, will in no instance bring out these values themselves....Socialization without humanization results in the weaving of the pall for the culture.[2]

Thus it is that the new social questions impel us to the necessity of humanization. If we would do that, says Noordmans,

> We are thrown back on God. He is no abstract individual, whose essence is exhausted in his work. He remains transcendent,

[2]   *VW* 1:214f., 220.

beyond his work. He still has the Spirit left. He is the overflowing fountain of all good. *We must seek a religious notion of personhood.*"[3]

God is thus the source of our personhood. Again Noordmans refers to Schleiermacher. "Like a potter he places the clay, the material of humanity, on the wheel of religion and shapes the forms of human personhood." Schleiermacher, originally a Moravian, grew up in a communion where a warm piety, focused on Jesus, was central and was deeply influenced by Romanticism. That movement saw everything, including personhood, as shaped by (and from out of) the whole. It stands squarely against the modern tendency toward specialization, which is inclined to "estrange the individual from the whole." Schleiermacher also thought along this Romantic line, albeit "more historically, more Christian." He provided a first impulse to what is so deeply desired, "a theory for the religious formation of the person." According to him, the individual is not derived from the whole (the communion); it is not determined, but it is "created through contact; it rises from within the communion." Thus, seen from that angle there is no contradiction between communion and personhood. It is just the other way around: "Communion creates personhood," and personhood is thrown into communion. Every person has her (accidental) reality, having originated and developed in contact with the communion.

Noordmans associates himself with Schleiermacher. However, he notes that Schleiermacher had incorrectly limited humanity in the sense that it was "all personal." Schleiermacher left vocational life, work, outside the picture. His view of life was too rosy. Calvin had a higher understanding. He saw the genuine individuality of every human founded in predestination. The human was chosen to salvation—indeed, in the most personal sense and at the same time communally. Calvin saw communion not only as a means for the human to receive salvation personally, but also as itself the embodiment of salvation. From Christ's death itself communion has already emerged. Humans are now bound with one another in Christ: that too is salvation. And salvation means humanity. From that perspective, human society loses its businesslike, impersonal character.

> Predestination (is)...a generating principle, an irrational basis, from which underivably, historically, individuality wakens, and not only individuality but communion as well, whereby both, individual and communion, maintain this character of

irrationality and underivability over and against each other, so that they cannot stand in the way of each other.[4]

Understood thusly, political and social relations no longer remain fixed, immovable, as though from nature. Calvin reckoned political and social relations as belonging to humanity. He advocated the humane, including work.

Noordmans also takes this position. "The Reformation (means) a *humanization* of life." Instead of sacramental powers, it put historical powers at the foreground, first of all the Bible itself. Consequently, the human could stand freely, personally, before God. In essence this was more revolutionary than the French Revolution. Today's crisis, Noordmans argues, is of a similar kind. Lines drawn in the Reformation are being extended. If in the Reformation it was still primarily about the human as person, it now is more directly about communion in which the person is not locked out but rather taken up. The "communal side" of life must also be humanized.

Here Noordmans sees a particular task for the church, but it must not desire to imitate the state. The state, of course, thinks spatially, in fixed schemes. It makes all equal, treats all citizens as the same, and so represses the person. In politics decisions are made through majority vote; the minority is shoved to the side. In the church it is often the same. Here, too, all is systematized, and differing opinions are seen as dangerous. Organizationally everything may proceed as if it were oiled, but "the religious person remains on the outside." It is precisely this person who must be made stronger. Her powers and gifts must be used in service of the communion.

How can the church be of assistance here? By becoming conscious of its character, says Noordmans.

> Not space, but time, history, (is) her element....The foundation on which the church is built is no statute, no constitution, but historic persons: apostles and prophets....As the state more clearly displays its spatial-schematic character, the church must consider its real element, history. It *must* give space for the person and cultivate and value the religious individuality....As it remains jealous of the egalitarian nature of the state, it will continue to kill the prophets and make martyrs. If the church will receive a "character," then the path to that end is not in the repression, but in the strengthening of religious individuality.[5]

---

[4]   *VW* 1:223.

[5]   *VW* 1:224f.

A development in this direction is helped by "the fact that labor is more clearly drawn into the notion of humanity." In general that is already the case; work "loses its nakedly business-like, indifferent, and spirit-killing character and demands a display of personhood." That already requires a connection of persons who are bound together but not identical with each other (like uniform dolls). Just as Paul sees the community bound with Christ as "an ideal, creating communion of labor," in which every member is "a new and free thought of God," likewise the church can and must have this in view. It always worships God's "free, spontaneous, personal, creating will." With reference to society, there lies within that as well "a rich program for the future development of the relation between communion and personhood."

Reactions

From letters that Noordmans received on the occasion of this lecture it appears that it was not experienced as easy fare, but "heavy food," "to be eaten in small bites." "It was somewhat difficult to understand completely as one heard it." But a number of responses offered warm agreement. "This is genuine ethical theology!"

One of the letter writers, himself a preacher and member of the Christian-Social Party (recently founded, a party that stood for a more social policy than was seen to be implemented by the ruling coalition of the time), said that he was struck by the relation of Noordmans's ideas and that of the party. He asked Noordmans whether he would not join the party. "I imagine that we could be able to have you as a member of the party."

How Noordmans answered remains unknown. One would suppose that he would not allow himself to be drawn into direct party politics. He was more a thinker than a popular speaker. But it is significant that his lecture gave occasion to such an invitation. One recognized the social tenor of his argument.

The Reorganization of the Church

At the close of his argument in "Communion and Personhood," we heard Noordmans make a few remarks on how the church must proceed: not systemizing, making all things equal on the basis of fixed statutes (or regulations), but built on the apostles and prophets, unafraid of differing opinions, with an openness to everyone's personal gifts. That the church of his time hadn't yet gotten that far was the starting point of these remarks.

He also engaged these matters expressly. It's already been mentioned that between 1911 and 1915 in particular he published frequently in the *Hervormd Zondagsblad* of the Friesian Preachers Union on relevant questions in the church. He was already busy with the questions he alluded to in "Communion and Personhood." His view of the church would necessitate a reorganization of the Reformed Church, and such was his plea in speeches, ministers' gatherings, and classical meetings.

He put forward as his reservation against the functioning organization of the church of the time (based as it was on the collection of regulations from 1816) that it "facilitates the parties." It is attractive as an administrative institution, Noordmans said. It cares that "each can possess what is private to himself (everyone for himself). With a careful, may we say fatherly, hand we are kept apart from each other." But such a church doesn't measure up! In the church it is to be the case that what everyone possesses is in "communion with all others." "The correct movement in the church is toward one another." Otherwise the church loses its reason to exist and the "dissolution of the church into parties" becomes imminent. It is to be remarked that in Noordmans's time the extreme right (the Reformed League) and the extreme left (modernists) within the church both found each other in this ideal and desired a common "division of the treasure" of the church. Noordmans warned that if one side prevails, the church collapses around us "as an instrument to reach the people." For precisely that reason, for the sake of the people, it is worthwhile to stand up for the church and to engage the battle for the reorganization of the church.

So too Noordmans entered a heart-felt plea for the national church.[6] He indicated support for those who put together and sent out a "manifesto for the Netherlands Reformed Church," who, over and against those who deemed the idea of a national church to be in conflict with a Christian conscience, had stated that "conscience *forbids* us from leaving the *volkskerk*." Writing in connection with the expressed desire to come to "an approach among the central groups of our church," through formulation of the faith that could function as a "greatest common denominator," he pointed out, in full sympathy with the suggestion, that not all church problems could be solved with a formula. He found that this threatened to become an ecclesiastical enclosure.

6   [Trans. The Dutch is *volkskerk*, or "peoples' church." This is not to be understood as the church *of* all the people, but *for* all the people. Hence it is the national church not in the sense that it is a state church, nor that all citizens are expected to be members. It is a church *for* the entire nation.]

The Lord finds himself *among the multitudes*. And his disciples may help serve the multitudes. The rumors, the suffering, and the heresies that surrounded him openly were less of a hindrance to him than many of us would want to believe.[7]

The church must take that to heart and not take heresies too seriously!

Noordmans would have nothing to do with an orthodox confessionalism that expects the salvation of the church through, if need be, the disciplinary maintenance of the confessions. And he would have even less to do with the adherents of the Doleantie, followers of Abraham Kuyper, who under the powerful motto "we Calvinists" desire a church "purified" of stains, a "confessional church," in the stead of a church which like a mother stands open for the people (*volk*).

Predestination—A Shift in Noordmans's Thinking

We saw that Noordmans spoke of predestination already in "Communion and Personhood." There, in the footsteps of Calvin, he argued that everyone's individuality and personhood, as well as his being united in community, is founded in predestination. God chooses humans personally and so unites them in a communion of salvation.

Predestination was a continual topic of interest for Noordmans. In 1921 he gave particular attention to the matter. His thoughts were published by installment in *Bergopwaarts. Weekblad voor Christendom en Cultuur* [On the mountain: periodical for Christianity and culture], an ethical periodical. Noordmans's contributions to this journal offer a glimpse of a more critical position he took on ethical theology's thinking regarding personhood. It was as if he started to tap a different keg. Predestination was no longer articulated as *founding* our (moral) personhood, but rather as something that *breaks through* it. This announced a shift in Noordmans's thought.

Many caricatures were (and are) in circulation about the doctrine of predestination. Calvinists, above all, debate the matter. Has God, from all eternity, already determined the fate of every human? Does the destiny of every person apply prior to her birth? And did God determine that destiny before the Fall or afterwards? Such questions are based on abstract, philosophical speculation. It is as if they must solve a logical problem. In fact, Noordmans says, predestination has to do with flesh and blood human beings; that is, humans in their concrete lives, with good and evil. Predestination, or election, is a word we use to denote the

---

[7]   *VW* 1:446.

"kernel of grace." It is an indication of "divine favor" that "liberates." Believing in election is "knowing...that when by our moral standards the world is lost, yet it is still not lost."

What Noordmans asserts as central to predestination is "that it brings our morality into confusion." Here human morals are broken through. We land *"jensets von Gut und Böse,"* "beyond good and evil." So the German philosopher Friedrich Nietzsche describes the *"Übermensch,"* the "true," strong human who has transcended all weakness and imperfection (and whom he contrasts with the average human, the weakling, who might seek comfort in religion). Noordmans uses this expression from Nietzsche in his description of what predestination means. At the same time he offers a contrast.

> In the Christian idea it is God's glory and strength that silences human right and breaks through human morality. In Nietzsche's doctrine the human himself breaks down the fixed limits. The Christian notion of predestination cultivates humility; the "Übermensch" bursts forth in pride.[8]

Despite this contrast, he regards their agreement as more important. "There (exists) in Christianity as well such a *"jenseits von Gut und Böse."* Note well that this does not end up in *im*morality! That would be the case if humans took to themselves the freedom "to know the difference between good and evil" (as Nietzsche's *"Übermensch"* does). No, in belief in predestination we are raised *above* our moral reflections, we come to a *"supra*-moral terrain." God's own self acts in God's own way that transcends our moral judgment.

Noordmans argues that it would, however, be a misunderstanding if we continued to think in terms of God's "power." That power is not purely arbitrary. In fact, the way that God displays divine power has a "moral content." For God's power appears as "liberating power." It liberates us *from* our morality. Not that we could exist without morality.

> Our moral notions are necessary to give direction to life so far as it depends on us. No one is entitled to consider that easily closed. And yet we cannot escape the feeling that human morality in one way or another holds us prisoner....Here God's predestination intervenes and wonderfully throws our moral notions into confusion....Our morality threatens to choke and suffocate life. Usually, human moralizing is boring....How liberating is

---

8   *VW* 2:126.

divine good favor here. In the world of his election these bonds are relaxed and loosened. The ban of our repression and hard judgment is broken open here. And giving ourselves over to this liberating feeling is better than being offended by it. The moment we do that we will know that election is not an arbitrary power but the highest morality.[9]

It is not only Paul (primarily in Romans 9-11) who talks about predestination; we also see it in the gospels, and there *in natura*. When Jesus appears, it *happens* that Jesus "lets it be known that he loves tax collectors and sinners and hates men of high degree." That cannot but evoke our objections. As we know, it does not mean that Jesus is indifferent toward the sinners and the righteous. No, he has "a preference for sinners." See the parable of the Pharisee and the tax collector (Luke 18:9-14): "The tax collector is of more use in the kingdom of heaven than the Pharisee." According to Luke's gospel (6:20), Jesus blessed "the poor"; according to Matthew (5:3), the beatitude concerned the "poor in spirit." Noordmans supposes that the latter is not a (later) spiritualizing or softening, but the original saying, in its most radical form. God chooses not only the *socially*, but even the *morally* inferior.

Our exegetes and commentators have difficulty with that. One is inclined to connect the divine preference for sinners with a presupposed "repentant attitude" and thereby make God's choice of sinners acceptable to our moral ideas. But then, in fact, one "breaks one's teeth" on the gospel. The fact remains that God's election, his preference for the sinner, means a "deadly stab in the legs" of our morality.

For this reason, predestination is rightly called the "heart of the church." It is the center of the gospel, even more so than the proclamation of the atonement. For it (specifically the notion that Jesus has sufficed for us in his death on the cross) is associated with our feeling of being set right. It articulates salvation in ways that we can imagine. It might even cause us to think that God needs a reconciling offering to be able to forgive us: which would mean that God cannot, as God's own self, really forgive. But the proclamation of predestination completely prevents such a thought from coming to mind. Here every accommodation to our notion of right, our moral consideration, is absent. Because of the proclamation of predestination we must (may) say that "God (is) so mild in the forgiveness of guilt that it offends us."

---

[9]   *VW* 2:128f.

"Believing on Authority"

In 1921, the same year that he published his views on predestination, another important publication came from Noordmans's pen, a brochure entitled "Believing on Authority." Here, too, he sounded new, critical, notes. Noordmans himself described the coherence between the two publications, noting that as "Predestination" argued "how God brings our morality into confusion," "Believing on Authority" argues that "divine truth disturbs our rationality."

It is a well-known expression that "we are brought to belief on authority." But, as Noordmans notes, the notion of "believing on authority" evoked considerable resistance in his day. "We do not easily accept something...because someone else says so." The thought behind this aversion is that "we think we know everything by ourselves." Of course at first we receive everything from others. But what someone else tells us becomes genuine truth for us when we have made it our own; in other words, when we understand that the other was correct.

That is true as well for modern theology, says Noordmans. In modern theology one strives to present matters of faith that transcend our understanding or historically precede our grasp, so that "we maintain that we ourselves have gotten behind them." So a good deal of use is made of the insights of the German philosopher Immanuel Kant. He broke with the notion that a human is able to know reality simply through reason, or theoretical insight. Indeed, he said, reality in itself (the *Ding an sich*) is unknowable for us humans. But, according to Kant, not everything is said therewith. Besides the theoretical capacity for knowledge, there is practical insight into what is good and evil, a capability to evaluate, to value, reality. Modern theologians find their connection there. They argue that a human not only has understanding but feeling and will. The last two work together equally well in the search for religious truth. If religious truth is at issue, they even precede understanding. That means that "although we cannot approach the highest goods through our understanding, we (can) still do so from the emotional side of our essence." That is, according to Noordmans, how the newer theology works, that it can still justify our religious knowledge as a "kind of knowing." We can even pretend to be "nearly absolutely autonomous" in our religious knowledge. For that reason there exists a crisis in preaching. For the preacher is, par excellence, "the other in matters of faith," and we can no longer abide being referred to the authoritative proclamation of an other.

Completely against this tendency, Noordmans appeals to another philosopher, the seventeenth-century French thinker, René Descartes. Descartes distinguished between the exact knowledge of natural science on the one hand and historical knowledge on the other. In the natural sciences it was about discovering for oneself, coming to a clearer insight by oneself, not parroting what others have said. In historical study, however, one had to follow what others have related. Descartes did not value the latter, historical study, very much, but found it to be second rank. The exact knowing of natural science was for him the highest form of knowing. With this reasoning, Descartes laid the foundation for rationalism—the thought that we come by reason to the knowledge of truth—as well as for the development and success of the natural sciences. Still, Descartes had an eye for historical knowledge in its own particularity as it relies on the word and the authority of others. It would be well if that element of Descartes's heritage would also be considered. Then the idea of "believing on authority," in other words, believing by virtue of revelation, would no longer have to sound so odd. Is the knowledge of faith also not historical knowledge?

Indeed, modern theology also talks about the "revelation of God." Does this still mean acceptance on the basis of authority, that is, on the grounds of witness about what has happened? That is not very clear. Take, for example, the resurrection of Christ. As a historical fact it includes a salvific truth. It is that truth that is the occasion for modern theologians to concentrate on the spiritual meaning of the resurrection. From there, one tries to "make it clear how we can still experience the resurrection spiritually and hence ourselves give *witness* to the historical fact. The resurrection in its moral sense becomes the cornerstone on which the resurrection in its historical sense rests." So here, too, the notion stands, "that we need no authority because we know it for ourselves."

In fact, the "old" and the "new," conservative-churchly and modern, "believing on authority" and "acceptance by virtue of our own insight" still stand over against each other. Yet, says Noordmans, the (conservative-churchly) advocates of "believing on authority" in practice pretend to know by themselves alone, while among the moderns, the "autonomy of religious knowing" is officially set on the throne. What is required is a "solid theory that teaches us that in history our agreement is required in a completely different way than in the exact sciences, and in which 'revelation' and 'authority' are properly respected." Thus, as with Descartes, we will have to be attentive to what is peculiar to historical knowledge. We must free ourselves from the thought that knowledge we receive from another is, as such, second rank. We must learn to understand that authority is a benefit. We have to hear the voice of another not only in our ordinary lives, but in the spiritual life as well.

We humans can make exact knowledge our own. But we also have moral notions. That is more. And as moral beings, we give validity to authority at the highest level of life, the spiritual life. Thereby reason is not made inactive, but it certainly acknowledges its lower position.

Believing is not only having a conviction. It also has a moral character:

> It is not only knowing, but trusting as well....We will naturally not give this trust to every authority. We do not acknowledge an authority that appears to us as immoral or unreasonable. No more than in political life. A decision is thus required from our side, equally as much the case as with exact knowing. I do not defend Romish immaturity here. But this I would defend, that when we have made this decision, we end by granting authority.[10]

This authority is not only the authority of the source, the story, the Bible. It is also the authority of witnesses, of the tradition of the centuries. In this sense Noordmans agrees with the word of the church father Augustine, "I would not believe the gospel if the authority of the church had not moved me to it."

Striking a New Course

About ten years earlier, in his discussion with A. H. de Hartog, we saw Noordmans advocate for the "historic character of the Christian truth." And in his earlier lecture, "Dogmatic Certainty," he had already turned against "rationalism that intends to be able to fabricate truth out of the naked intellect." Thus, what he put forward in "Believing on Authority" was not completely new. Still, he had not argued so powerfully before that God's truth "disturbs our rationality," because that belief, Christian existence, depends on that which comes with authority from elsewhere.

Later, looking back at the year he published "Believing on Authority," Noordmans would write, "At that time autonomy still enjoyed the upper hand in ethical circles and the brochure...gave occasion for a spirited discussion in our ethical study circle." Noordmans had begun to strike a new course. It was a course that would bring him into contact with new theological developments.

---

[10] *VW* 2:149.

CHAPTER 6

Theology in the Midst of Crisis

Laren

At the end of 1922 Noordmans accepted a call to his third congregation, Laren, in Gelderland. After more than twenty years, his ministry in Friesland came to an end. On March 25, 1923, he was installed in Laren, There, in the *Gelderse Achterhoek*, he would remain active for the final twenty years of his ministry, when he would retire.

Noordmans experienced his transition to the new environment positively. In answer to a greeting card, he responded in advance of his move: "The solution appears to us favorable. Laren is nicely situated and it appears to be a pleasant congregation." We have seen that his time in Suameer had been difficult. In his final sermon there, he shared a bit of that difficulty, not as a complaint but as a sober reflection.

> I am thankful that my work here has had something genuine about it; there was not only agreement, but conflict as well. Let me say it the other way around: not only hate, but love too; not only working against each other but also with each other. Still,

was it more of the first? Perhaps! But love and working together are like gold. In the black ore, here and there is a small vein.[1]

However that may be, in Laren he entered a different climate, less conflicted, more kind-hearted. Or, as he put it, "friendly." A friend and colleague called his move to Laren "a pleasant change of life, for which you will have thanked God's good hand." Nearly five years after his beginning in Laren, in the sermon on the occasion of his twenty-fifth anniversary in ministry, he looked back on his first years in Laren with gratitude.

> I can safely say that I find myself at ease among you. Many of your faces have become extraordinarily sympathetic to me. I value your dignified reserve...your mildness in your judgment of persons, your living grasp of preaching.[2]

Relations appeared to be good with the church council, wardens, and teachers as well; Noordmans typified them as "warm." What a difference from the situation at Suameer!

Later, in his sermon on the occasion of his fortieth year in ministry the tone remained positive.

> I thank God that I may say that I have no regrets over my twenty years as preacher in Laren. Here, before this audience, thoughtfully correct, I can best develop the ideas of Holy Scripture. Nearly one generation of elders and deacons have gathered around the pulpit during these years. They have always been a friendly and helpful presence.[3]

His ministry was not without tension and regret, however, even in Laren. Here as well as in Friesland, as Noordmans himself knew, that had to do with his peculiar disposition. For him, personal companionship was not an easy thing; that's just the way he was. In a letter to K. H. Miskotte he wrote something of this, although he put it in general terms: "We Hollanders (! – Blei) always have difficulty with house visitation. There is something of a réveil necessary to get us over the bridge." He would say something of this in his farewell sermon. "Perhaps I have been a bit stiff and reserved with you....You would have desired more warmth." Nevertheless, relationships here were not seriously damaged.

---

[1]   *VW* 7:416.
[2]   *VW* 7:423.
[3]   *VW* 7:429.

In contrast to the two Friesian congregations, at Laren he needed to lead only one church service per Sunday. Church attendance was (and is) not as customary in the Achterhoek as it was (and is) in Friesland. "I never got accustomed to that," he would later remark. On the other hand, his catechetical lessons were inundated—that also was (is) part of the way of life in the Actherhoek. Weekly, he had three to four hundred catechists, a "powerful host of young people." He saw that as a great privilege and experienced it as a joy "to regularly receive those young, attractive, open faces." The large weekly classes must have cost him a good deal of time and energy.

While Noordmans had had little contact in Suameer with colleagues in the area (Suameer belonged to the circle Drachten), he was soon invited in the Achterhoek to become a member of the ministers circle there, the "Rainbow." The circle gathered regularly, often in Zutphen, but also, by rotation, at the homes of the members. Invariably one of the members would lecture, but fellowship was also an important element. Noordmans went happily and actively participated in the group. "The Rainbow" became for him a circle of friends. Here he experienced a "piece of isolation removed."

Four months after his move to Laren, a third child was born to the Noordmans family, Johannes Arnoldus.

Kohlbrugge and Barth

In the previous chapter we saw that Noordmans's thought had worked its way through a shift at the beginning of the 1920s. Having begun as an ethical theologian, attuned to the meaning of human personhood, he developed into a critical theologian who put emphasis on the fact that God's coming to the human, as an authoritative intervention, disturbs human morality and reasonability. He went further along these lines during his years in Laren. He came into contact with new, foreign, theological thought that was of the same critical sort. Specifically, he encountered (what he called) "Swiss theology," as developed by Karl Barth and those of like mind. Noordmans saw it as his task to bring this theology to the attention of his ethical circle.

The first time he referred to this theological direction was in a lecture that he gave April 21, 1925, at a gathering of the Netherlands Reformed Preachers' Union; he published it the same year in *Stemmen voor Waarheid en Vrede*. The subject was "Kohlbrugge's Significance for Contemporary Theology." Noordmans naturally mentioned Barth here, in whose thought he saw a strong relationship with Kohlbrugge's theology. Perhaps it had been Barth's influence that had convinced

Noordmans of the relevance of Kohlbrugge's theology. This, then, was the reason he was so eager to put Barth on stage in this lecture.

Hermann Friedrich Kohlbrugge (1803-1875) was in his time a misunderstood, lonely thinker. He shared the Réveil's criticism of the lukewarm nature and disinterestedness of the then official Netherlands Reformed Church in matters of faith and confession. His critical attitude was even the reason why he (originally a Lutheran) was not admitted to the ministry of the Reformed Church. On the other hand, he did not agree with the emphasis that groups within the Réveil placed on the necessity of personal conversion and sanctification of life. In contrast to their emphasis on experience and mysticism, he placed the accent on God as the sole center of the human. A human must not climb above himself to come "closer to God." No, it is precisely the human as he is, as creature, as sinner, that is, as "flesh" (and not as "personhood"), who is the object of God's mercy. Jesus' incarnation meant that he became *flesh*, in the sense that he himself became sin. Therewith he became our representative. That, and not our own struggle to holiness, makes us new humans. Experiential circles eagerly wanted to know when (precisely) a person's conversion took place. Kohlbrugge maintained that even conversion remains outside ourselves; it took place at Jesus' cross and resurrection. "I was converted at Golgotha." There was absolutely no place in the Réveil for this radical emphasis on the objective nature of salvation. Ultimately, Kohlbrugge went his own way. He was minister of a free congregation in the German city of Elberfeld.

Noordmans had already expressed himself concerning Kohlbrugge. But while Noordmans had grown up in a home deeply influenced by the ideas of the Réveil, in his lecture of 1925 he is more emphatic and more positive on Kohlbrugge than he had been previously. He notes that Barth's theology reminds him strongly of Kohlbrugge's. As Noordmans puts it, Kohlbrugge desires to know nothing of "small religion" (i.e., morality, knowing good and evil) in the context of salvation and puts all his emphasis on "great religion," the grace of God who comes to the human for nothing, but that he may, precisely as sinner, believe. The same is the case with Barth; he too deems that all is dependent on God's grace and mercy. Barth agreed with those who typified his theology as a "theology of the absolute moment." The Word of God comes to be here and now and destines me for Christ. It all comes down to that. Barth appears as a Kohlbrugge redivivus." Only he thinks more radically, more "rashly consistently," along the same line.

In essence, says Noordmans, that is more the line of Luther than of Calvin. With Calvin and Reformed Protestantism, unlike with Luther, there is a sense that the sanctification of the believer is an event of "ever firmer developing continuity" by the work of the Holy Spirit. That coheres with a different way of thinking about the meaning of Jesus. The Lutheran tradition sees in Jesus primarily the act of incarnation, God's self-emptying. There is, according to Noordmans, no real space for a view of Jesus as a human. In the Reformed tradition, however, there is space.

> For the Reformed Jesus is much more an individual person who also exists for his own sake. He has a particular place in creation and has in it an office, a work to do and maintains that place as the Head of humanity....In Reformed theology Christ is not a *place* where divine and human nature...temporally meet each other, but a *person*, in which both are perpetually united.[4]

Thus, there is also space for a vision of the believer as a human who "becomes a person in the full sense in sanctification." The qualification, "theology of the absolute moment," Noordmans grants, does not apply to Reformed theology; "the continuity of regeneration has priority over the hearing of the Word as a momentary event." Hence, the Reformed take the "burden of culture" on themselves. "Personhood" is a cultural notion. "So the Christian ethic develops, the small religion which intends to lead the way through culture to the *parousia*" (i.e., the Second Coming, the completion).

In this typification of the Reformed position we hear again the word "personhood," a word that was so important to Noordmans as an ethical theologian. He leaves no doubt that he finds himself in the Reformed camp. He adheres to the notion of the "spiritual life morally and culturally mediated."

Nonetheless, at the close of his argument he advocates the "awesome" theology of Kohlbrugge (and Barth). He defends it against mischaracterization and misunderstanding, as if this "theology of the absolute moment" would not take account of creation. Noordmans argues that it in fact does! It sees the creature, the unspiritual, as a "motive for God's mercy." It is only the valuation of experience and the effort involved in salvation through works that "taunts creation," an attitude that leaves creation irreparable. And so, according to Noordmans (in 1925!) this theology responds wonderfully to the conditions of the time.

---

[4] *VW* 3:519.

European cultural life stands in the midst of a profound crisis, and in the trenches the personal is forced back to its natural basis. Those who went through this school have re-learned the meaning of being "flesh." So both, personhood and culture, are forced back into our consciousness.[5]

Even apart from that: are the Reformed not too inclined to see the kingdom of God as the completion of our culture? Does their thought not threaten to become "an overwrought fixation of the continuity in the life of faith (think of Abraham Kuyper, who interpreted regeneration in physical terms!)? Noordmans asks,

> Have we not to remind ourselves in contradistinction that the Word of God alone remains to eternity, even though that may sound Lutheran? We will not recklessly rid ourselves of small religion, which is ordered by God for humans, to find ourselves in great religion. But we may remind ourselves that the last includes the first. Ethical religion has its borders.[6]

Advocate for Barth

If in the lecture discussed above Barth is mentioned secondarily, a few months later Noordmans made him the direct object of consideration. He did so in a lecture on Swiss theology held July 21, 1925, as part of a conference of the Ethical Union. This lecture, along with contributions from others of the "Barthian school," was published in an expanded form through the study commission of the Ethical Union. Noordmans here typifies the theme of Barth's *Römerbrief* (interpretation of Paul's letter to the Romans).

According to Noordmans, Barth's theme is "the unknown God." One can correctly speak of Barth's agnosticism, so long as one sees that it is an agnosticism "filled with faith." We do not know God, and that includes knowing God in and through our culture, because it is the case that we are "much more known by God." It is this reversal that Noordmans indicates as characteristic of Barth's theology.

This reversal immediately implicates a second theme in Barth's *Römerbrief*. It consists in what Noordmans calls "the contraction of the image of life." Paul (like the Credo) has Jesus' "historical life" disappear between the significance of his birth and death. Jesus is not a "religious genius" for him, but more the "*object* of God's holy Council," "handed

---

[5]   *VW* 3:525.
[6]   *VW* 3:525.

over for our sins and raised for our righteousness" (Romans 4:25). Well, says Noordmans, Barth views our human life in the same way, "not as the subject of the knowledge of God, but as the object of God's knowing." Seen that way, it is the case that in Adam we are sinners, in Christ justified. What we call "person," "culture," interiority," or "character" plays no role here. Noordmans did not hesitate to remark (for his ethical listeners!) that Barth "comes into opposition here with some forms of ethical theology in which all rests on personhood and culture."

Still one cannot, Noordmans clarifies, call Barth's theology hostile to culture, for Barth is not about the negation of life or culture as such. He views our life, with all its morality and culture, as placed under the judgment of God. God judges us as sinners and nonetheless as justified (as Jesus is "made to be sin" by God's judgment and is justified). This double judgment of God, in Barth's vision, declares life in its continuity and moral development as not inferior; rather, he impresses on it a divine predicate.

With this last move Noordmans turns immediately to the third point that he will emphasize as characteristic for Barth. Barth sees everything as dependent on this one, double judgment of God that condemns and sets free. That means that the human does not reach salvation through a gradual transition "from the state of sin into the state of righteousness." God turns himself about and intends now to "know our life no longer as sin." This graceful judgment is "creating *Neuprädikation* [new predication]"; it creates what it expresses. "So then the turn of our life is in God and not in us." Hence the salvific meaning of the "contraction of the image of life."

In this way, Noordmans expanded what he had alluded to in his earlier lecture on Kohlbrugge. And he did so with apparent agreement. He was primarily interested in bringing Barth's intention to attention. Just as in the earlier lecture, his conclusion was positive. Noordmans presented himself as a strong advocate (in his own, ethical circle) for Barth.

In Discussion with Barth

That is not to say that he did not have his reservations. He aired them a number of times, particularly in his text, "Swiss Theology." He remained an ethical theologian standing in the Reformed tradition. It is not that we know God, but that God knows us;—assuredly, that is at the outset. But what is the case now with "the birth of morals and culture" as it emerges from "being known"? We must speak about that as well. But, says Noordmans in 1925/26, Swiss theology has thought very little about that. *That is its weak point.* Barth

> avoids...indicating how...our moral and cultural life is set in motion between the poles of God's judgment. Thus with him... the moral process is somewhat empty. When the right relation is restored and the way is not from our thought to God's thought, but the other way around, through faith, then a relation between the two originates again. When the divine dialectic, through its holy tension, creates a moral field in which ethics and culture become possible, then the two react in turn against theology and modify its contradictions. There is then more space for the doctrine of the Word than has been created for it by Barth.[7]

Barth rightly begins with God's graceful, judging Word. But the point is that the gospel proclaims that "the Word has become flesh." Noordmans means that the Word is aiming at expansion, at taking shape in life, including in ourselves who are touched by that Word. That Barth in his *Römerbrief* devotes no thought to this is, in Noordmans's judgment, a shortcoming.

In the same year, 1926, Karl Barth visited the Netherlands for the first time. He had a meeting in Amsterdam with a small circle of leading Reformed theologians. Noordmans was also present. He did not allow the occasion to go by without putting his reservations about Barth on the table, and these were not easy for Barth to answer (as Noordmans would remark four years later in a reflection). J. J. Buskes, a Reformed minister in Amsterdam, later noted in his memoirs his recollection of this meeting. "I shall never forget how Barth listened to these questions with great thought. He said that he had never had such questions put to him as those from Noordmans, questions that he frankly acknowledged as on target." Barth himself wrote about this to his friend Eduard Thurneysen. He called Noordmans the one "who stands apart from the others, and of a higher caliber."

A Theological Authority

Noordmans had become an authority in theological Netherlands. Correspondence that has been preserved shows how he was consulted time and again on theological questions, including by those who had considerable intentional theological study. Editorial boards of

---

[7]   *VW* 3:581f.

theological journals invited him to join them and were greatly honored to publish articles from his pen. Noordmans did not have a doctorate. Nor would he later enter doctoral studies and the writing of a doctoral dissertation, although there were those who encouraged or invited him to do so (as for example, A. Eekhof, a professor at the University of Leiden, who wrote to him: "Frankly speaking, I find it too bad that a man of your gifts and capacities would not be promoted.") But the lack of a doctoral title did not lessen the esteem in which he was held in the theological world of the Netherlands.

A number of times in these years his name came up in searches for church professors. That was already the case in 1923, when a vacancy opened in Groningen (where, ultimately, Th. L. Haitjema was named as the successor to W. J. Aalders). In 1926 it occurred again, this time more seriously. There was a vacancy in Utrecht. Noordmans, by then aged fifty-five, was one of the three official candidates proposed to the synod. His candidacy drew a lot of attention, including in the public press, and found approval. But the choice of the synod went to the young M. van Rhijn. One of Noordmans's friends wrote, disappointedly, "I hope that you continue to publish....Our church has still too few dogmaticians.... You come the closest!"

The hope of this letter writer for more publications from Noordmans's hand would not be disappointed.

A New Time Demands a New Theology

In the second half of the 1920s, Noordmans dedicated considerable thought in different publications to the significance of the Ethical Party and its theology. That milieu had shaped him from the outset. His new insights, developed in contact with the "Swiss theology," provoked him to a reconsideration of his own theological milieu. What is essential to the Ethical Party? What possibilities does it offer for development in the direction of the new, critical thought?

He let no one doubt his connection with the Ethical Party. In a reflection from 1926, he pointed out the difference between this party and those in the Reformed Church who led the fight in the Confessional Party. The interest of that party lay in its conservative character; the confessionals, in contrast to the "watered down liberal theology" of the beginning of the nineteenth century, had rightly asked consideration of the "treasures which are given in the confession of our church." But, so Noordmans argued, this conservatism is at the same time its weakness: the confessionals want to remain faithful to the old without following its consequences for the present. They are mainly *against*. They turn against what others develop in a new theology, but they offer no new theology of their own.

The latter test, the attempt to offer a new theology, is assuredly met with the leaders of the Ethical Party. For them it is less about maintaining existing, classical doctrines (formally and juridically) than "placing themselves in the force field of the moral energy that the church's confessions brought into existence" "and discovering then the horizons of the new world which opens up in the confession." This description by Noordmans brings to mind what would be formulated later in the 1951 church order of the Netherlands Reformed Church: that the church (today!) confesses—not in *agreement*, but "in *communion* with the confession of the fathers." At that time, with the establishment of its own confession, the church entered a way—the "way of the church's confessing." Now the issue is, as the later Reformed Church order states, to proceed on that way, in that track (as Noordmans put it: in that "power field"). This was precisely the program of the Ethical Party as Noordmans had sketched it in his reflection of 1926.

There have always been considerable misunderstandings about ethical theology, Noordmans maintained. One misunderstanding was the notion that this theology would lay special emphasis on the *application* of the truth. One derived this notion from the idea that doctrine, our understanding of the gospel, was and is an established fact, and that the question of how this doctrine works itself out in life is a separate matter. That is what is "ethical." But what genuine ethical theology is about is that truth itself is "ethical." One does not only look from doctrine to life, but also from life to doctrine. The "application" is deemed to work backward on the truth, the understanding of the gospel. Doctrine, or dogma, appears different then; it is "no longer a point of doctrine" but becomes song, praise. This all means that "whoever does not know the Christian life also does not know Christian doctrine.... Truth and morality are one." That is what the founders of the Ethical Party, D. Chantepie de la Suassaye and Gunning, intended.

In 1926, Noordmans considered himself to be a spiritual partner with them. At the same time he saw limitations, shadow sides. Had the ethicals perhaps related truth and life too directly? Must we not consider that there may be more distance between the two? Does not truth also stand over and against life? Gunning certainly understood something of that. And today, said Noordmans in 1926 prophetically, that has become clearer still.

New chasms have opened themselves for our generation and we can no longer see the cosmos as harmonically as he did. In his view, everywhere the lightning of Judgment strikes through the forms of life. But this lightning strike holds something immanent: it looks like fire from cloud to cloud, from form to form....Now the Judgment has touched the life forms of above and we have to take account of that theologically.[8]

A new time demands a new theology. Did Noordmans see the crisis of National Socialism already on the rise?

A Quest for a Theology that Takes Account of the Crisis

That Noordmans had the "Swiss theology" in mind in these considerations, especially as developed by Karl Barth, remains unexpressed. In a later, broader evaluation of ethical theology this theology was indeed referenced, though in the context of Noordmans's argument on which (what kind of) theology is needed for the present. He published this reflection in 1930 and thereby ended for himself, and in his own mind, a phase of reorientation.

As a characteristic of ethical theology as it appeared in the nineteenth century, Noordmans pointed in this reflection to the endeavor to connect with the philosophy of the spirit (developed by the German thinker Hegel). That philosophy interpreted progressive world history as the process wherein God is active realizing himself as spirit. In this vision God, the world, and the human do not stand over and against each other as points in a static triangle, but God is dynamically present in world history. Chantepie de la Saussaye was inspired by that philosophy and would fill out the vision from the standpoint of the Christian faith. That faith also speaks of the coming of God into the world, in Christ, through the Holy Spirit, a coming that happened once, not to be repeated. Therefore, Christian faith is the true "philosophy of the spirit."

This is impressive as a theological undertaking, but it requires a great deal of care. In this formulation, the gospel too easily becomes encapsulated in a philosophical system. The founders of the Ethical Party had to struggle continually against that danger, but they were not able completely to avoid it. Noordmans's conclusion to a full overview was that the "unity of life" rules too strongly in ethical theology. The relationship between the world, the human, and God is taken "too

---

[8]   *VW* 3:388.

organically." The emphasis on life is so strong that thereby the "faith is nearly squeezed out of theology."

Ethical theology spoke gladly and primarily of the "idea of personhood" (we saw earlier that this idea was dear to the early Noordmans). Over against the rising materialism of the nineteenth century, the ethicals believed it was important to emphasize that the human is more than what is determined by the material world. Human life is living in freedom and on the way to freedom! They understood the gospel in this sense. At the same time, this accent is inclined to forget that judgment is laid against human life as well, and that the gospel concerns itself with just that. Of course, one is aware that all is not perfect. One knows about sin and about the law of God. Still, that a crucial relationship between God and humans exists, that a "violent eschatology," a powerful intervention of God in human life, is necessary in order that all will come out right—that is not considered. That the gospel is critical of human life is not, in Noordmans's judgment, sufficiently accounted for in ethical theology. It was too much about "creation and humanity" and too little about the cross and judgment.

Was there still a future for ethical theology? According to Noordmans, there could be, but only if it became more aware of being rooted in the Reformed tradition. That meant that ethical theology must never be satisfied with appreciating particular groups of interested "intellectuals"; it could not remain a "theology outside the church and the life of the people," for Reformed life touches the society, and so it intends to do. Ethical theology had become somewhat elitist. It was not popular, had few adherents. But that should not remain so!

> If ethical theology, following its period of impopularity, does not make a dialectical transition to a period of broader expansion... then it must be reduced to a hobby of a few groups of intellectuals. I deem that danger not at all imaginary. It is specifically called to provide guidelines for preaching, which must call broad parts of the population of our large cities back to Christ.[9]

But that does not mean automatically taking up again "the historic inventory of the Reformation." The Heidelberg Catechism, for example, was in the past an excellent "example of guiding the gospel to the heart." But does not this catechism also have

> more or less the characteristic of what is common in the spiritual life of a particular group, of a particular societal position? Its

[9]   VW 3:470.

psychology demands free time and the custom of self-analysis and its gratitude evokes, as an undertone, the thought of a peaceful societal position. Perhaps one can obtain a view of the future of ethical theology by considering the question of whether it can be used as a book as much for a people's church [*volkskerk*] as for a middle-class church. Does it provide sufficient expression to the ever growing tension between the gospel and the masses? The entire truth is effective at every point, Gunning remarks somewhere. And I would wish that somewhere in the midst of it...the fiery gong of the Spirit would flash through the book.... And will church discipline, which may never be completely lost in Reformed life, not have to take on completely new forms, now that the "corpus christianum" of the Middle Age, for which Calvinist discipline intended to be a compensation, lies hopelessly apart?[10]

Ethical theology must give account of such questions, Noordmans argues. It was not mistaken in its search for the "unity of life." But it comes down to how this unity is understood. We do not have a simple, direct, natural entrance to the mystery of creation (e.g., via magic), or to salvation (e.g. through mysticism). The judgment of the Spirit stands in between. It is the Holy Spirit who opens for us the meaning of creation and salvation in its preaching of judgment and justification. One has always been conscious of this in the Reformed tradition. And that is what gave and gives the Reformed life of faith its sober, simple character. We humans, who would be lost if left to ourselves, are set by the Spirit into salvation in the preaching of the gospel. Thus

> It is not certain that a group of confessional or ethical persons offer more for theology than a non-churched neighborhood. Who will say how the "kingdom of heaven" has come near with the "crowds who do not know the Law?"[11]

That too means the unity of life; but then with a different content: unity through judgment. With a theology that takes account of that,

> the ethical preacher will have an indication of a broader and deeper entrance into modern life than when Christianity and culture are identified in one way or another or when Christianity is sought in personhood.[12]

---

10 *VW* 3:470.
11 *VW* 3:471.
12 *VW* 3:480.

We recognize in Noordmans's argument the emphasis on God's speech that judges and creates, the same emphasis that we heard from him earlier concerning Barth in the lecture, "Swiss Theology." Here, too, he refers to that theology—and adds his critical notes thereto. Its strong point, Noordmans says, is that it is a "theology of judgment"; only it should not forget that the judgment that God speaks through the Spirit means for us new being, new life. Theology as knowledge of God's judging action may and must also be knowledge of the fulfillment. From that perspective Noordmans finds the "Swiss theology" unsatisfying.

At the same time, we see here how Noordmans was active in delineating a theology that would be able to enter deeply and broadly into modern life, a theology in which the work of the Spirit would be central.

CHAPTER 7

The Thirties: Augustine

An Active Life

In the 1930s, a time of crisis in Europe, Noordmans was at the peak of both his activity and his productivity. Having turned sixty in 1931, the pastor at Laren was active on many fronts.

At that time, the struggle for the reorganization of the Netherlands Reformed Church came to a head. Earlier, while still in Suameer, Noordmans had been involved in it. Then his concern was for a proper understanding of the role of the minister. In 1930 he became engaged more directly in the struggle for reorganization both strategically and theologically. As a prominent member of *Kerkopbouw*,[1] which was established in 1931 and worked for both the reorganization and the renewal of the church, he offered his contribution from his parsonage in Laren.

---

[1]   [Trans. Along with *Kerkherstel*, *Kerkopbouw* advocated for the reorganization of the Netherlands Reformed Church. *Kerkopbouw*: "the building up, or edification of, the church," and *Kerkherstel*: "the reestablishment of the church," will be left untranslated.]

At the same time he probed the theology of the church fathers and the Reformers more deeply. In particular, he was busy with Augustine. He had been so earlier, but Augustine was being memorialized in 1930, fifteen hundred years after his death. That provided the occasion for a number of anniversary celebrations, and it gave Noordmans the opportunity for renewed study and publication. He held a number of lectures on Augustine, and, in addition to a number of articles, he published a separate book in 1933.

More general theological matters engaged Noordmans's thinking during this period as well. His thoughts on these matters became known to a greater audience when he collected a number of his lectures and essays—noted in the previous chapter—with some other writings and published them in 1930 under the title, *Geestelijke perspectieven* [Spiritual perspectives]. D. Tromp, a minister in Zandvoort, who along with Noordmans was one of the first to introduce "Swiss theology" in the Netherlands, was one of many who responded to the writings. "Your whole collection, your style of writing, is singular. You write as though for yourself....your style is that of someone who formulates thought for himself, and had the fortune to do so with striking images."

The primary fruit of his theological reflection during this period, his book *Herschepping* [Re-creation], appeared subsequently, in 1934. In it Noordmans presented a brief theology in outline.

It was no surprise that at that time his name continued to surface in connection with professorships that were becoming vacant. In 1931 it was about a vacancy teaching philosophy of religion at Leiden. When Noordmans did not make the short list of candidates, it elicited this comment from an insider: "What you lack is traditional connections." In 1932, there was again a vacancy in Leiden, this time for a church professor of dogmatics. Noordmans was named but again did not make the short list (he had become "too old," and F. W. A. Korff was appointed). In 1934, there was a vacancy for a church professor in Utrecht (for biblical theology, dogmatics, and practical theology). As in 1926, Noordmans's name was one of the three proposed. At the beginning of 1935, however, the decision was not in Noordmans's favor (S. F. H. J. Berkelbach van der Sprenkel was named). He was not unaffected by the decision, and many correspondents also expressed their regret. G. van der Leeuw, a professor in Groningen and Noordmans's comrade in the struggle for the renewal of the church, wrote: "It is perhaps cold comfort, that you mean more as a rural pastor in Laren for church and theology than a number of professors put together....Don't stop working. Your work is valued by very many as the best that we have and certainly as the most original." The synod's policy for appointments held no expectation for this sort of originality.

Notably, in that same year, 1935, the University of Groningen conferred on Noordmans an honorary doctorate in theology. It was given on October 16. Professor W.J. Aalders, Noordmans's promoter, said on that occasion, "Precious gold requires minting. So I deem it a privilege that we are able to acknowledge your scholarly achievements in this way. This tribute does not create something that does not exist, but acknowledges what does." In his remarks on receiving the honor, Noordmans's gratitude included his delight "that the senate of this university...encourages me to continue. Whatever else the title might mean, it includes a clear task to teach." Continue he would.

In the following chapters, we will consider Noordmans's activity in the three areas noted above. In this chapter, we discuss Noordmans's study of Augustine. We will see that his theological reflection and his involvement in the struggle for the reorganization of the church already echo in it.

Augustine

Augustine must indeed have engaged and inspired Noordmans a great deal. Augustine (354-430), bishop of Hippo in North Africa (then a Roman province), was also a theologian involved in the church. Like the twentieth century, the fifth was a confusing time. The Roman Empire (at least in its western half) was about to collapse. Augustine experienced the plundering and defeat of Rome. That plundering and defeat meant the end of an entire period of culture. Would all the values that the empire had brought to bear be lost? The Christian church is to be thanked that such was not the case. Says Noordmans, it "fulfilled the vocation to receive and absorb the invasion of the barbarians spiritually." Noordmans sketched Augustine as one who offered considerable assistance in this respect.

What Noordmans saw embodied in Augustine was that the presence of the church is important for society. Noordmans himself was deeply convinced of this same importance. What was happening in Russia and especially what was taking place in Germany during that period, the 1930s, held his attention. It evoked in him the notion that the church is to be church, and not simply an association (a confederacy with an administration). The church must involve itself in society. In May 1933, he spoke at a meeting of *Kerkopbouw* in Deventer and drew parallels with the events of the fifth century.

A few kilometers east of this old commercial city a great tragedy is unfolding. It is first of all the Jews who are involved, not only as hypermodern men, but as descendants of old Israel. The intention is to destroy the Old Testament and purify the New. The church must lend itself to execute this religious operation on the ground of a political biblical criticism such as the world has not yet known. It is as though we were transported to the days of the population movements when the Rhine was the frontier and the flood from Russian and Germany rose which overwhelmed Latin Christendom. Then the church was young; it survived. It is now old and shows a number of signs of crumbling. Will it survive? In the German church *race* has steadily overtaken the gospel. One experienced there a flood of *blood vis à vis* the *Spirit*.... We must again learn to think ecclesiastically...from the kingdom of God and the rule of Christ.[2]

According to the report of this meeting (probably put together by Noordmans himself), Augustine was expressly on his mind in the final sentences. Augustine's ideas about the kingship of Christ, Noordmans argued, must be at the forefront once again. The report notes that if that does not happen, then "Europe returns to the beginning of its history, that was one of revolution and tyranny....Politics without the church runs aground. Where church folk no longer exist, there will be no folk. The church, not the race, forms the nation....The Germans can learn that from the Jews."

The State as a "Band of Robbers"

Noordmans's book, *Augustine*, appeared as a publication of the *Volksuniversiteitsbiliotheek* (Library of the people's university). During his time at Suameer he had given courses for the People's University (specifically at the local unit in Dokkum). This book likely grew from a similar course.

It is a historical study but very relevant to its time. It devotes thought to the turbulent course of Augustine's life. How, following a "short puritanical" youth, he came into contact with philosophy. How subsequently he became an adherent to Manichaeism, a movement that saw evil localized in the body and the bodily. How, having freed himself from that movement, he left North Africa and established himself first in Rome and later in Milan and threw himself into a career as a brilliant orator and teacher of rhetoric. How he became aware of the

---

[2]   *VW* 5:203f.

significance of the Bible and of the church under the influence of the bishop, Ambrose. How it was primarily the letters of Paul that pointed him down the road to Christ and taught him the distinction between philosophy and biblical proclamation. How that, thanks as well to his mother, Monica, led to his conversion and break with his past. How he, baptized by Ambrose, returned to North Africa shortly after the death of his mother, with the intention of establishing a cloister with his friends. How he then, during a discussion of that enterprise while in Hippo, was chosen by surprise by the city populace to be the assistant to the bishop in that city. How he was ordained in 391 as presbyter/coworker of the bishop (his tasks being catechesis and preaching), became bishop himself in 395, and remained so until his death thirty-five years later.

Augustine described the course of his life in his *Confessions*, itself cast as a confession before God. Noordmans gives a short discussion of this book but concentrates on Augustine's most important writing, *De Civitate Dei*, [On the city of God], written between 413 and 426 as a commentary on the plundering of Rome, a foreshadowing of its defeat. For Noordmans it was not about the person, but the bishop and church father Augustine.

In Augustine's time a clear distinction already existed between the eastern (Greek) and western (Latin) half of the Roman Empire. Since 380, Christianity had been the official state religion in the Latin half of the empire. Beneath the surface, however, a form of paganism continued to stir as a romantic honoring of Rome's glorious past and with the allure of its pose of openness to all and its aversion to all sophistry in the service of truth. That was the situation that faced Augustine, Noordmans says. In contradistinction, the bishop maintained that world history is a contradiction and struggle between two kingdoms: on the one hand is the kingdom of self love (which forgets God) that persists in a refined, subtle paganism, and on the other hand is the kingdom of the love of God (which forgets the self), represented in the Christian church. It is this contradiction between Christianity and paganism that Noordmans highlights and deems important for the present as well.

Augustine starkly compared the relationship between the kingdom of self love and that of the love of God to the relationship of a robber state *vis à vis* the kingdom of grace. He typified the first in the following famous passage, which Noordmans cites:

> What are states other than bands of robbers written large, when justice has disappeared? And on the other hand what are bands

of robbers other than small states? For in the latter case as well there is a group of men, organized by the authority of a ruler, bound through common arrangement; and the booty is divided in mutual agreement. When through time the troop of evildoers has grown, so that one starts to occupy fixed positions, establishes places to live, overcomes cities, subjects the population, then it takes...the name of a state and it has that to thank...not to the fact that its desire to plunder has lessened, but that it has become immune to punishment.[3]

Noordmans comments,

We have here one of those dangerous expressions, whereby a peaceful citizen keeps heart and which one still comes across with prophets, apostles, church fathers, and reformers. They bring us into the presence of a duel that is happening between heaven and earth, and articulate the critique of the gospel on the world...the lightning of the gospel (strikes) the entire field of the political world history.[4]

Of course, Augustine was thinking concretely of (the history of) the Roman Empire of his day. There he saw "pride and vanity reveal themselves, against which the church father will place humility and truth, which the church knows."

For Augustine it was "a question whether good order is possible outside Christianity, and he denies it." He saw the state as by definition inspired by gods and spirits. What had earlier been honored as personal gods were later seen as personifications of abstract entities: Victory, Fame, Prosperity, Virtue. You still see something of that, says Noordmans, with Roman peoples.

One does not adequately learn the words "victoire" (victory) and "gloire" (glory) from a dictionary. You discover what is embedded in them in the *Marseillaise*. They are goddesses who lead the army to the Rhine. They still have to do with the essence of the state. Augustine's book can teach us how difficult it is to separate state and paganism.[5]

Augustine intended to ban these "gods" in his book. They are not realities but idols. How could the Roman Empire then remain so great and powerful? Noordmans gives voice to Augustine's answer:

---

[3]   *VW* 3:87.
[4]   *VW* 3:87, 90.
[5]   *VW* 3:93.

The God of the Christians, the God of the Old and New Testament is the one who has made Rome great. His real work is to give humans eternal life, but this is also his ordinance. Thus world history is radically turned. Rome loses its claim to be the head of the human family....The humble God of Judea, of Golgotha, is the Lord, whose throne supersedes Rome's glory. Augustine writes... his book to show the power of humility. So...the whole course of Rome's history (gets)...its meaning from the gospel.[6]

That is the same nation that we earlier heard described as a "band of robbers par excellence, when justice has departed."

The Church: Holiness, Authority and Catholicity

The events of the 1930s, particularly in Germany, provoked Noordmans to read Augustine's evaluation of the state with deep interest. Was not the state there, in Germany, manifest as a "band of robbers"? And the current state of the church with which Noordmans had to do compelled him to read Augustine's vision of the church with a similarly deep interest.

Augustine spoke of the "holiness" of the church. For him the church's holiness could not simply be found in, for example, the purity of its members. Rather, he saw it connected with Word and sacrament, through which God's Spirit works. Thus, because Word and sacraments are administered in its midst, the church can, with all that it lacks, be called holy. Holiness has nothing to do with philosophical eloquence. In connection with the church, holiness is better denoted as "love." The church is not a kind of philosophical school.

Augustine had also gradually developed a view that there is an *authority* in the church. Originally attracted by Manichaeism and philosophical rhetoric, he had later learned that faith is based on something else. He put it pregnantly: "I would not believe the gospel if the authority of the catholic church had not brought me to it." He had met that authority in the shape of the bishop Ambrose. In his preaching, Ambrose had directed Augustine to the authority of the Bible. Conversion was, for him, an act of subjection to higher instantiations. This subjection was for Augustine not a proof of spiritual fatigue. Indeed, it gave him new courage to think. In Noordmans's focus on this element of Augustine's view of the church we recognize the author of *Geloven op gezag*, from 1921, which was discussed in chapter 5.

[6]   *VW* 3:95.

When he became a bishop Augustine was confronted with a schism that had appeared in North Africa, as it would later elsewhere. The schism occurred at the time of the last persecution of Christians, the beginning of the fourth century. It had originated out of protests against what some saw as an indulgent attitude of the leadership of the church toward the Roman authority. Those in opposition had separated (as the "donatists," named after their leader Donatus) and formed a counter-church. Over and against this fanatic opposition, Augustine advocated for the unity and *catholicity* of the church. The true church is not to be realized through schism, he argued. Schism emerges from pride, but love is the bond of the church. The church is catholic; that is to say, it is "not from one people." By Noordmans's account,

> There is a sphere beyond the personal, beyond what is particular to every holy group, where the things of God receive their final authority. One must stand there to receive the full salvific enjoyment of God's grace. And whoever is given an office in connection with the power of this grace does not lack the authority of the office on account of personal shortcomings. In contrast a schismatic church...lacks the salvific power in its offices and institutions, because it lacks the spirit of love, which can work only in the full entirety of the catholic church, where angels and humans extend to each other the golden scales of God's grace.[7]

For Augustine, Noordmans says, the "personal and the national retreat in the presence of the catholic." Thus, there is "also a place for the figure of Peter in papal form." Of course Augustine doesn't dwell on that particularly. One could hardly imagine him doing so. The great catholicity of the universum, as he developed it in *De civitate*, "intervenes too powerfully in the earthly." Later popes like Gregory VII and Innocent III "turn his book in this direction." In contradistinction it was Calvin who took up Augustine's ideas on the church and its holiness and the church of love and worked them out in his own way. "The great *volks* churches in Calvinist nations intended to be catholic churches without a pope."

Over against the reality of the Roman state (as it was being dissolved), Augustine posited the reality of the kingdom of God, represented in the Christian church. Here two sorts of citizenship stand in opposition. Only where that is understood can the gospel be spoken. Whoever wishes to maintain an unbroken development "from Adam"

[7]   *VW* 3:146f.

lands unavoidably in the "band of robbers," with Rome as a symbol of the state and humanity as its highest exponent. The narrative of history becomes gospel only when in contradistinction from the procession of kings and Caesars the procession of prophets and martyrs comes into view.

As he wrote on Augustine's understanding of the church, the church of Noordmans's own time, including the church in the Netherlands, must have been in his mind—more an association than a church, without authority, and without a conception of catholicity.

CHAPTER 8

Re-creation: An Original Theology in Outline

Re-creation

Noordmans's original theological vision took on clearer contours in the 1930s. This was particularly the case with the book noted in the previous chapter, *Herschepping* (1934). We will consider that book in this chapter.

It emerged from Noordmans's contact with the *Nederlandse Christen-Student Vereninging* (NCSV) [Dutch Christian Student Union]. Established in 1896, the union had chapters in every university and organized (Bible) group studies for students. It also arranged regular student conferences, and it organized summer camps for students in secondary school for which university students (NCSV members) provided leadership. For these students NCSV work often meant a fresh encounter with the Christian faith. Considerations of personal piety and engagement with the Bible accompanied openness to social and international issues, all in an ecumenical spirit.

Noordmans had contact with the NSCV as early as the 1920s. He gladly found himself on the speakers' rotation for conferences. He wrote many articles for the NCSV publication, *Eltheto*. So too he received an invitation from the leaders of the union to write something that could help leaders of biblical studies and summer camps when, for example, they had to present religious addresses (outside, in tents, in any case "outside ordinary church settings"). The result was *Herschepping* as a publication of the NCSV.

The book presents itself as a "compact theological guide." In fact it is, for all its brevity, a complete dogmatics, the only work of this sort that Noordmans would ever write. As a minister of a congregation he was caught up in the practical work of the church. It is true that he had also become more and more involved in discussions of what was at stake on a broader field, in church and society. In that connection he had emerged as an authoritative speaker at regional and national meetings and as a publicist. But what he wrote was always concerned with current events. His reflection and study sought answers for questions that people, himself included, saw as concrete. His views in general were short and to the point. They bore an aphoristic character. He simply had no time for complete theological publications. Perhaps we must add that he was not inclined to make the time.

All in all Noordmans wrote only a few wide-ranging books. One of them is *Herschepping*. But, as has been indicated, that book too had a concrete occasion. In it, no less than in his much shorter papers and articles, he wrote with an eye to the practical. The origin of this book is typical of Noordmans's publications. He offered a dogmatics, but one aimed toward preaching. In fact, he said (and knew himself in line with the Reformation) that dogmatics is to have proclamation as its goal, for dogmatics is not a matter of the school but of the church.

"According to the Gospel
God Can Always Do Something Different"

The distinction between school and church was important for Noordmans. He emphasizes this point immediately in the introduction to his book. The school is about philosophical thought. It functions according to its own insight. It sees all things in a logical or scientific or psychological context. It soon comes to see "God," "world," and "human" as three separate subjects. But particular human logic does not rule in the church. There one knows himself, together with others, as bound to a rule. In the church it is not about giving expression to original beautiful thoughts as they emerge but about the proclamation of the gospel. That cannot happen randomly. Everyone who must give a religious address, even if it is "outside ordinary church settings," has to consider that in so doing he finds himself in principle "in the church."

The rule that applies here is what is ordinarily called "dogma." That rule, says Noordmans (we recognize here the author of *Geloven op gezag* from 1921), has authority. Its basis is "that God has said it." Others have heard it before us: reformers, church fathers, apostles, prophets. An echo of what they have said will resound through our speaking, when it is good. The deadly sin in science (plagiarism) is normal here: "We constantly borrow in a sermon." In science we derive one thing from another, but the preacher reckons with God as the real Speaker. And "every word of God's revelation is an other and with each other word the Speaker comes closer."

Not that the intention would be to proclaim church dogma as such. In fact, as Noordmans intends it, dogma is a sort of watchdog, sleeping in the church when nothing is afoot, waking only when things threaten to go amiss in preaching. Proclamation is not about dogma but about the Word of God. And that is ever new: always that "which must be said now." A preacher who would summarize dogmatically "correctly" the entirety of Christian truth in every sermon is in fact a record player. No, "in the sermon the entirety of dogma is drawn off-center. Otherwise it cannot *work*." "We do not preach everything carefully at the same time, but one thing with power."

Thus we do well to keep in mind the movement, the "plural," in God. "According to the gospel God can always do something different....When speaking is not sufficient, he comes; when coming is not sufficient, then he comforts." In this way Noordmans points to the dogma of the Trinity, "God reveals himself as Father, Son and Holy Spirit." This dogma sounds scholastic, but it was in fact a decided rejection of scholastic thought. The church was taking care that "the school did not ruin the truth of the church."

Christian Life on Earth

In a separate chapter, Noordmans considers what it meant for Christians when they realized that the end of time, the second coming of Christ, was not about to take place. One must "no longer" learn to live as Christians "only for eternal life...but also *in this life*," a complete change. Earthly life is given weight. The church must set itself to such matters.

This does not mean that the church can lose itself completely in society. It maintains a certain reserve, an "asceticism." This is a matter of course; isn't the church in its essence headed toward Christ's second coming? It "cannot germinate from a natural root. It cannot stand on the foundation of blood and race." It has its own origin and vocation.

In any case, it was this necessity (experienced primarily in the western church) to involve itself with earthly life that led to the fact that, besides the confession of faith (the Apostles' Creed, the short liturgical summary of faith), a catechism gradually came into existence, instruction for how Christian life on earth can take shape. In that regard, Paul could still limit himself to "a few practical remarks at the end of his letters." But in the catechism, besides the content of the Christian faith, command and prayer were explicitly handled. Against tendencies that emphasized that humans have the capability to lead a good Christian life on their own (in "asceticism"), the emphasis had to be put on grace. That can, according to Noordmans, best be described as the "accompaniment of Father, Son, and Holy Spirit in time," and so as an "indwelling in feeling, a leading in life" (we already noted that Noordmans deemed this to be underemphasized by Barth). It is in the sacraments, in baptism and the Lord's Supper in particular, that Christian life is given shape; that too is dealt with in the catechism.

A kind of dogmatics soon came into existence as well, "a more scholastic way of expounding Christian faith." This was not without danger; nevertheless, it was sometimes necessary to defend the gospel against unbelievers or to teach it at a university.

Dogma in the Reformation

In the Reformation, dogma became a matter for the congregation itself. A new type of confession of faith (or confessional writing) originated, broader than the classic liturgical form; a kind of short, simplified dogmatics. The ideas of "justification by faith" (particularly in the Lutheran tradition) and of predestination (particularly in the Reformed tradition) were emphasized. Predestination "does not derive our destiny from our essence, nor our salvation from our virtue," but "finds its ground in God's goodness." Even if it is not spoken of directly, it is there in the background of every sermon, when all is well. Young people ("the casual scholar now out of doors...in the tent") sit with life questions: Whereto? Why? The message of God's free election is the answer. And justification by faith does not mean that we must present faith as a condition for salvation. No, faith is "the good work, surprising both ourselves and God, that is reckoned to us as righteousness."

The classic confession of Father, Son, and Spirit appears to be shoved aside in these Protestant traditions. In fact, Christ stands more clearly at center here. He, the Word in person, addresses us. This, Noordmans argues, is not about a visibly imaginable historic Jesus. It is about Christ "clothed in his gospel," the crucified, broken one, who is proclaimed to us by the Spirit (bit by bit)—as we see it primarily in Paul's letters.

Faith in God the Father

Noordmans handles theological material proper as he follows the classic dogma of God's Trinity: God the Father, the Son, and the Holy Spirit. However, the way he deals on the one hand with the work of God the Father in direct connection with the work of the Son, and on the other hand places great emphasis on the otherness, the peculiarity, of the Spirit and his work with regard to the Son, is very particular. He sees a greater connection between the Father and the Son, between the Son and the Spirit a greater distinction, even a greater distance, than Christian tradition and theology generally suppose.

As to the first, Noordmans resists the general notion that belief in God the Father is different from belief in God the Son; as if belief in God the Father would be self evident; as if it could be made to be possible and acceptable philosophically. In fact, Noordmans says, we already are retreating from that in "our time" (he refers implicitly to Barth's Swiss theology here). We are learning that we cannot speak of God the Creator without immediately speaking of Jesus the Savior.

> The creation that science handles is not the real creation. It is an abstraction. In the true creation we come up against sin, suffering and death, of what the Jesus of the Apostles' Creed is about. Creation is full of scandal...of itself it yields paganism, not belief in the Father....When we take creation not as completed whole, but connect it closely with Christ..., then it is not a dark chaos or a self-ruling Greek cosmos, but a spot of light around the cross. And in that spot sin becomes manifest...God has created things good; more than that the Bible doesn't tell us. —Thus we must not try to approach creation as a quasi-infinity or quasi-eternity. We quietly leave the millions of years of the universe and biological life to themselves....We keep ourselves near the cross.... The Bible itself teaches that creation is a critical concept. It begins with creation but without telling us anything further about it. It only says that all was good. With that we have a measure in hand to see that all is fallen. The Bible itself immediately begins with the story of the fall and the Old Testament tells us nothing more than that fall....So it appears that the confession of the Father and that of the Son, the Creator and the Savior, belong together. The God of Joseph is the same as the God of Jesus. He makes good

to come out of evil. He creates light from the darkness of sin. He is the God of the resurrection behind the cross. Thus when we speak of God the Father, Creator of the heavens and the earth, we do not need to teach astronomy or geology. We also need not speak of human capability: thought, feeling and will....We do not have to do with this "school" knowledge here. The confession of the Father...makes us think of the fall....With that, we stand in the midst of everyday life, in the refuse of all the days, in daily failures, in the newspaper reports of world events, the stories of fall after fall, that make it difficult to believe in the Creator....All belief in the Creator must be born from that.[1]

Creating Is Dividing

Is Genesis 1 then only a background, and is what the Bible has to tell only to be heard in the stories that begin with Genesis 3, about the fall? No, "creation" as a "critical concept" already emerges in Genesis 1-2, says Noordmans, in the creation story itself.

When we say the word "create," we often think of beautiful forms, of harmony, of an unbroken whole. We think that it is through seeing or living with such forms that we are able to come into contact with God the Father. We walk with him in the rose garden. However, the Bible has us see something else. In the beginning God created the heavens and the earth. That is the first great division. It is the act of a spirit; a judgment.—That repeats itself with the days of creation. Light and darkness, day and night are divided. The waters above from the waters beneath. The sea from the dry land. Then with the creation of the human, Eve is divided from Adam. And there follows in the prehistory (Gen. 3-11), beside the line of promise, which already emerged then, a violent description of creation outside Christ. In a continuing series, we see the transgression of Adam and Eve, the revolution of Cain, the work of Lamech and his sons, the war dance for Ada and Zilla, and the disaster of the flood. Thereafter follows a failed attempt to storm heaven.[2]

Noordmans does not fail to note clearly the relevance of all this.

---

[1]   *VW* 2:245-47.
[2]   *VW* 2:251f.

> Outside Jesus Christ the riddle of creation contains only horror....
> The eighteenth, nineteenth, and twentieth centuries cohere as
> they exhibit something of that horror.[3]

That creating is dividing and not forming, seen biblically, means
that we must disabuse ourselves from thinking that "salvation" would
mean the "reparation" or "restoration" of creation.

> Often one maintains that we must speak of creation as a
> complete, finished work of God. It is done...and a harmony rules
> in the whole, which one must attempt to discover....All is good
> and our life would be perfect and happy if a small disturbance
> had not appeared, which we call sin, with another disturbance as
> consequence, death....Thus, one makes of the gospel an episode,
> while science, art, and politics allegedly would deal with the real,
> serious work of creation. The work of the Father, the *making* of
> things is then considered completed and the only thing that now
> matters is the re-establishment of its harmony. In expectation
> thereof one retains a *ground* under foot and that has a greater
> bearing power than the foundation that Jesus Christ has laid. The
> human has blood *in* his veins and that determines his existence
> more foundationally than the blood of Jesus Christ that has
> flowed *for* him.[4]

"Ground under foot," "blood in the veins." Noordmans points
here (as he did earlier when speaking of the church that cannot exist on
"the foundation of blood and race') in passing to what was happening
at that moment (1934) in Germany. Hitler's National Socialism, as the
glorification of the German race and the glorification of "blood and
soil" of the German people, was actively growing there. And it is being
applauded by the "German Christians" who see in Hitler's appearance a
new beginning for Germany and Christianity given by God. Noordmans
was convinced that this was "creation faith," which cannot possibly
appeal to the biblical proclamation of creation. Such views do not
understand that creation itself is touched by sin, that "sin extends as far
as creation." Thus, "a beautiful world, an honorable human, a wondrous
soul, that we cannot use in a sermon nor in dogmatics." Where the
"forms of creation" present themselves and "coincide...outside the

---

[3]   *VW* 2:251.
[4]   *VW* 2:253f.

gospel," we are dealing with a new paganism—and "the beautiful loses a bit of its beauty" (an understatement!).

Biblically speaking, creation is not something finished, complete. It "accompanies us until we arrive at Golgotha." There we see just what creation presents. Hence Noordmans's earlier expression, "Creation is a spot of light around the cross." With that, he intends to say that at the cross God's creating judging, his "creation" as "dividing" reaches its climax: God himself enters judgment; he enters the fall.

That means that whoever would venture a "doctrine of creation" cannot do so other than through the telling of a story, the story of the "procession to the cross." It is the same story that is told as the Old Testament continues. You could put it the other way around and say that the entire Old Testament is the story of creation. In God's work is embedded "progress, notwithstanding sin." God's creation, i.e. his judgment, pursues the fall "all the way to Golgotha"; we read that in the Old Testament. "God himself (enters) the misery...and heals the (break)"; we read that in the New Testament. Thus, just as the Old Testament (in its entirety) narrates the creation, so the New tells of the incarnation of the Word. But then one should realize that the incarnation does not mean a (beautiful, new) formation either; precisely as creation is not formation. Creation is broken, fallen: in just this way it connects with the incarnation.

> When we say that Christ has become human, it is not intended that he gives us to see how the *original* world has been. The emphasis falls on "the likeness of *sinful flesh* (Rom. 8:3)....It is the emptied creation for which He has emptied himself.[5]

Belief in Jesus Christ

In his chapter on belief in Jesus Christ, Noordmans explores these last words. Jesus is human, but in such a way that he sees creation, as it were, "from below." He knows the "underside of the boards of the world's stage. He feels himself at home among sinners and the sick"; that is his humanity. In fact, as the gospel describes it, his entire appearance is about the cross and resurrection. "Jesus has suffered 'the entire time of his life.' And the resurrection accompanies his journey. Wounded and dead we see rise." For that reason, you can distill no "Life of Jesus" from the gospels. The gospel certainly includes history, but it is a history of an entirely peculiar character. It is a history that cannot

[5]   *VW* 2:257.

be described; it can only be preached, as we see Paul do it in his letters.

Only when we keep this in mind, says Noordmans, can we concentrate fully on the human side of Jesus without reserve—as the western church has always done. This is best done when the Reformers' scheme is followed. They referred to the Old Testament and spoke of Jesus' "three-fold" office: prophet, priest, and king. This is important for the church. For

> preaching must also take account of feeling and life. Prayer and commandment are also dealt with in the church and in catechizing because the church is being granted continuity over centuries. We do not only say as Christians...*I believe*, but also, *I pray*, and *I live*. The doctrine of the three offices provides occasion, then, to spread the content of the gospel...be it in a very fragmentary way, over our life. In the strict sense the *gospel* has no continuity; it is a reversal. But the *gospels* certainly have continuity, and in that they are a parable of the life of the church.[6]

At hand in the pattern of Jesus' three-fold office we can also be alert for wrong turns.

> In an account of Jesus' teaching, we will be protected from moralism as we are reminded of his prophetic office. The temporal nature of the Old Testament priesthood will warn us against sacramentalism and episcopalianism in the discussion of Jesus' suffering, against being swallowed up in mysteries and solemn gestures. And the rule of the royal office will restrain our preaching from mixing Christianity and culture.[7]

Jesus' Humiliation and Exaltation

On the other hand, it is particularly on great feast days that preaching can find greater support from a different pattern of thought: distinguishing between Christ's humiliation and his exaltation in the course of Christ's journey. As Noordmans has it, that helps us see the gospel as what it also—or even primarily—is, i.e., "as the great reversal in which God breaks through time and life." This pattern of humiliation and exaltation also best reflects the shape of the Apostles' Creed.

Noordmans discusses in turn the stages of Jesus' life as they are distinguished in the Apostles' Creed. Regarding his birth, "One must

---

6   *VW* 2:274f.
7   *VW* 2:276.

read Luke 2 in connection with John 1 and vice versa." His birth was "incarnation." That is something other than a neutral "becoming human." We must, Noordmans says, not "remain here in the personal, the biological, sphere." To do so is to understand Jesus' appearance as the "direct continuation of creation" as form. He could then be imagined as the "highest exponent of creation..., the ideal human, the god-man." Sometimes, as for example in the Roman Catholic Church, one sees Christ's incarnation as something that extends (via the church) all the way to salvation. That is incorrect. The incarnation has happened once; it does not proceed of itself but is continued (discharged) by the coming of the Holy Spirit.

It is striking that immediately following the mention of Jesus' birth in the Apostle's Creed, his suffering is mentioned.

> If the incarnation were a continuation of creation...in a creaturely, pagan sense, then this sequence would be incomprehensible. Then we would expect the worship of the god-man following the confession of the incarnation. And then the life of Jesus would follow the birth in the Apostles' Creed. That life would then have had to be treated as a revelation of divinity; an apotheosis of which lay hidden in the mystery of the birth.—We find nothing of this....Thus in our preaching we may make Jesus no hero or martyr or saint; still less a beautiful soul or pious believer, and least of all a social or cultural phenomenon. Jesus is the *Savior* of the world....He is not the flower of creation, but he is himself God, who has set himself in our place, who has followed us in our fall. He is the Son, through whose person and work we know well that the Creator is truly a Father.[8]

Where the gospel is viewed through the framework of humiliation and exaltation, as in the Apostles' Creed, there, Noordmans says, "suffering must be seen in closer connection with salvation than with atonement." Moreover, it must be considered that the Father himself is involved in the suffering of the Son. Only so can the world be helped.

> Even God cannot help the fallen world without participation in its suffering. The world is not to be helped directly. Creation does not proceed directly to a kingdom of God....In the incarnation God as Sufferer stands over and against God as Creator. The Son also takes the indirect consequences of the Father's creation

[8]   *VW* 2:280f.

on himself. Judgment, through which the fall, the knowledge of good and evil, is propelled to Golgotha.—And these indirect consequences of creation in the Bible are called the real creation.[9]

The old church understood Jesus' "descent into hell" in a cosmic sense. "Hell" was seen as the underworld, the world of the dead. The Reformers could not go along with that. But, Noordmans supposes, we have a better understanding of this cosmic aspect in our time.

> In a time of apocalyptic aspects, preaching cannot really allow itself the luxury of making an article such as this inactive. The world since the Renaissance and the Reformation has not become so humane that it may limit the deepest and the worst to the human soul. Suffering and death also are of cosmic dimensions. "Christ in the trenches" is not a subject for preaching that our age would not understand.[10]

Jesus' resurrection and ascension are stages of exaltation. The resurrection does not mean that Jesus "still" continues to live, as though he were immortal. As though that would be a necessary consequence of his death! No, "Resurrection means to say that God, following the cross and death, the grave and hell, is still Creator." God delivers a new judgment, so that Jesus rises. And so "all the suffering of the world is changed into hope."

In the Apostles' Creed all the stages of humiliation and exaltation lead to the article on the Holy Spirit. "The incarnation (is) from beginning to end destined...to be taken up in the work of the Holy Spirit." Just as the creation cannot be understood outside the incarnation, so the incarnation (the entirety of the facts of salvation in Jesus' way) cannot be understood if it is not "submerged in the Spirit of Pentecost." It does not proceed of itself; its continuation is the work of the Spirit. That is to say: it must be *preached*.

Jesus' Three-Fold Office

At the close of this chapter, Noordmans gives further consideration to the other pattern, that of Jesus' three offices—the prophetic, the priestly, and the royal. With the prophetic office, Noordmans notes that biblical prophecy "is a public action. It addresses the multitudes, the poor in spirit...Jesus is the friend of tax collectors and sinners." That

---

9   *VW* 2:281f.
10   *VW* 2:283.

public character coheres with its absoluteness. This prophecy is not concerned with the incidental; it is not, for example, a "brilliant insight on one area or another of creation." Indeed, "it engages the most central matter: our salvation, our eternal relation with God." It does not forgo the one who expresses it. "Jesus himself becomes the victim and he interprets it with his life and death."

Jesus fulfills his prophetic office when he relates parables and when he performs miracles. Each "parable contains a mystery that waits for its disclosure until the coming of the Holy Spirit." And the miracles are "parables in action." As with the parables, what happens in the miracles is about the kingdom of heaven. "Simple help is insufficient in this world." Here salvation happens, and it "is not restitution but re-creation."

Consideration of the priestly office puts the preaching of the atonement at center. The letters of Paul, more than the gospels, are its charter. We do not get a direct connection to Jesus, not even via the gospels. "The Comforter replaces him."

However that may be, Jesus' suffering is about more than his utter faithfulness to his mission. Terms like substitution, punishment, and offering cannot be ignored. It must be proclaimed that Jesus has undergone punishment in our stead. Otherwise, the "preaching of atonement does not have integrity." It is true that here again a certain asceticism, or reserve, is necessary. This sort of atonement language can be only provisional, useful "so long as the eschaton remains outstanding."

As to the royal office, says Noordmans, we see it already in the gospels, as for example in Jesus' appearance with power against evil spirits. But it is there primarily in "Christ's rule through Word and Spirit, as it emerges from the exalted Lord. In any case, Jesus' kingship cannot be proclaimed too directly. Consider that "Jesus' appearance, what was visible, recedes, originally with the resurrection and then completely in the ascension" and that the story line about Jesus "finally leads to the outpouring of the Holy Spirit."

Belief in the Holy Spirit

That there is so often little awareness of what is peculiar to the Spirit is understandable given the kind of work the Spirit does, according to Noordmans. God the Father stands as the Holy One over and against us sinners. The Son has come near to us, even beneath us, but a distance still remains between him and us. But the Spirit "comes still closer to us than the Son." "To make the works of the gospel truth and reality in us, that is his office. The final reach of the Word, that which touches and converts the heart, that is called Spirit." So the Spirit appears "to become one with our heart." "All that the Holy Spirit is and does...appears to have no other existence than as human spiritual life."

In the Bible, however, we are taught that the Spirit's presence and works are not exclusive to the human heart. The Spirit does great, more-than-human things: "the breathing of creation, the inspiration of Holy Scripture, the preparation of the incarnation, and the calling of the church." The Spirit is thus more than means and instrument. He is himself divine Person.

In the central passage of his book, Noordmans calls the entire work of the Spirit "re-creation." Earlier he typified creation as a critical concept; God's creation means his judgment on us. Creation is characterized by sin and death. They "can only be checked when God follows us into the fall and places himself under judgment. That is the work of Jesus Christ." Hence the entire human condition in the gospel, at the cross: misery, guilt, death, everything at a standstill. The work of the Spirit in the present is that life returns:

> With the resurrection of Jesus it begins. It is...God's judgment on Christ's work....Piece by piece everything in Christ's work is taken and proclaimed to us (John 16:14). Everything is seen differently. The deaf hear, the blind see, the lame walk, dead are raised, the gospel is proclaimed to the poor. The impasse under judgment, misery, the guilt, death come to an end. The Spirit hovers over the valley of dry bones. (Ezek. 37:1-14)[11]

This is again creation—creation as recreation. Here it is said again, "It is good." And that means now something other than becoming cognizant of the fall; indeed, the fall is now excluded. A judgment is delivered on us again, the judgment of the Spirit. And that

> makes the sinner just, the fallen a saint. It gives all things a new predicate—here too creating is dividing. The Spirit divides the old man from the new...in re-creation the critical character of creation receives its completion. Then the distinction between good and evil is no longer a fault but a virtue. The new man casts off the old in conversion.[12]

---

[11]   *VW* 2:300.
[12]   *VW* 2:300.

Grace, Justification, Regeneration, Belief

In this connection, Noordmans considers what "grace" means. Often, grace is presented as though it connects with nature. That would mean that the work of the Spirit, re-creation, would have to be conceived as a "semi-betterment of the work of the Father." No, says Noordmans, the Spirit is not one to make improvements, a repairer. He is "as Re-creator...a Creator in the full sense and creates out of nothing. Unless one would wish to call sin and death 'something.'" Grace is not a "something" that could then be added to the natural; "grace" is more "the summary name for God's judgments in re-creation and the communion of the Spirit. Judgments that emerge from the eschaton and set everything right in the completed work of Jesus Christ."

At its core, that is called justification by faith. Thereby we are pointed to the Spirit. In the gospels we read that Jesus offers blessing and makes blessed. But without the Spirit, what is narrated in the gospels remains limited to those who are addressed there and then. It is still only a parable of the comforting of those in misery. It becomes reality precisely in the work of the Spirit. And "in justification by faith God also is justified. Therein he comes to his honor." Here too the "real works of God" come to bear. All else, all that preceded—cross, birth, death—they are "finally His unreal works. In the creating word of justification God himself gives new names to things and proper names to his children."

At the same time, the theme of justification may not be isolated from the entire work of the Spirit, which includes regeneration, conversion, vocation, sanctification, Christian life. However, one does not wish to hold strictly to a particular order, for then dogmatics again becomes a scholastic system. And sanctification should not be conceived of legalistically.

Concerning regeneration (Noordmans here refers to "the revived Calvinism of the nineteenth century"), it may not be made something mystical, unconscious, "a vague hypothesis beneath the sermon or the sacrament, a point of anxious supposition for faith, an audacious underpinning in politics and science." Then we would again proceed from the incarnation as an event that continues forward (as hidden). Regeneration is, biblically speaking, a future conception; it "includes the complete renewal of the world." "Deriving belief from a seed, a human capability, that is implanted in regeneration, that is a scholastic way of thinking that does not belong at home in church." No, "regeneration is a promise and must continue to be an address that fits in one connection with justification by faith."

When speaking of faith, Noordmans says again, "Belief and authority belong together. Not the idea but the work wakens faith." Hence God's judgments expressed in the Word

> surge through...our existence in a manner that extends far beyond the reach of understanding, feeling, and will....We believe not only with that small bit of light of a particular hue that we call our understanding....All that exists in time and eternity can be laid on the scale of our conviction. Biblical saints have believed with their bodies equally as much as with their spirits, with their sin as much as with their holiness, with their deaths no less than with their lives. In scripture, belief is not that precise, the correct activity of the citizen as it is sometimes taken to be. It is often rough work that can only be recognized as faith by God or a prophetic eye.[13]

We will later hear how Noordmans, in a meditation from 1946, "Sinner and Beggar," on poor Lazarus (Luke 16) will say that he "believed with his wounds, with his total misery."

This expansive understanding of faith coheres with the breadth, the all-encompassing nature, of the work of the Spirit. Thus, says Noordmans, "The church has, by the mouth of its greatest representatives, then, always drawn a margin of faith *around* the church... there are 'sheep who are not of this fold' (John 10:16)."

Sanctification

Finally, Noordmans speaks about the Christian life. There is between faith and life, he says, "no real boundary." The Christian life is also not "a given thing."

> Attempts to unite Christianity and nationality, Christianity and culture, Christianity and morality with each other, will never completely succeed....The relation between gospel and creation, gospel and race, gospel and humanity, gospel and culture, gospel and morality, must always be introduced critically, in preaching.[14]

The critique that the cross and the faith bring has "certainly relaxed but is never forgotten" in Christian life. "Justification always moves into sanctification," however, this does not mean that sanctification would "cease to be a graceful reckoning by God." "Sanctification does

---

[13]   *VW* 2:311f.
[14]   *VW* 2:314.

not become a peculiar merit. It is living on justification and waiting upon glorification." The relationship between creation and re-creation is again at issue here. If re-creation would be the "restoration of the given creation," then the particular task of the believer on earth would be given great emphasis. Too great an emphasis.

> That the believer has a task is true, but it is a child's task. It is more play than work. It is an imitation of God's work and it continues to be true that the work is completed...The task of the believer has no *direct* relation to the eschaton. He will have to turn from his work to God's.[15]

But even so sanctification retains an important place in preaching, something to which, says Noordmans, the Lutheran church gave too little thought. The believer may not simply be left helplessly behind in his life as a citizen, in the "sinful order of creation." To do so would be to grant independence to nature, *vis à vis* grace; that must not be allowed to happen.

Cards on the Table

Thus far we have sketched the contents of *Herschepping* in outline. With this book Noordmans has (apparently innocently) summarily and decidedly laid his cards on the table. We will see how he will draw the lines more sharply in his later work, particularly on the peculiar work of the Spirit.

---

[15]   *VW* 2:316.

CHAPTER 9

Passion for the Church

The Struggle for Reorganization of the Church

As noted above, the struggle for the reorganization of the Netherlands Reformed Church came to a climax in the 1930s. Noordmans played an important role in that process.

The existing church organization had been put in place in 1816 by royal decree. At that time, shortly after the upheavals of the French Revolution (1789) and the French takeover of the Netherlands, the new, once again independent Dutch government (King William I) saw the church and Christianity as vital factors for order and peace in society. The king himself had authorized the proposal of a new "General Regulation for the administration of the Reformed Church." According to this regulation, the church would be led not by ecclesiastical assemblies (consisting of office-bearers, representatives chosen by the church itself), but by small, appointed administrative bodies. They were given old, trusted names (synod, classis), but in fact they formed a new, dictatorial administrative system. That system had been retained even when, following the constitutional changes of 1848, the influence of the king, i.e. the state, had been drastically reduced and the church could stand on its own feet.

According to the General Regulation, the new "synod" had the task of organizationally minding the store. It was to take up as formal a position as possible. It was definitely not to involve itself in such matters as questions of faith or doctrinal differences. Were it to do so, it was supposed, the order and peace of the church, its unity, would be disturbed. The synod held to this instruction.

The classic Reformed confessions were not scrapped. However, the General Regulation did not explicitly state that they were to be seen as authoritative. Certainly one still talked about the "doctrine" of the church and that it had to be "preserved," but what that included was stated nowhere in the regulations.

The notion that leaving fundamental, substantive questions aside could facilitate order and peace in the church, however, appeared to be an illusion. It was precisely that neutral, formal policy which over and over again provided occasions for considerable trouble. At stake was the question of whether the church would have to be reorganized so that it could again become a confessing church. The regnant system allowed the contradictions noted above (chapter 3) between "confessionals" (orthodox, advocating official recognition and maintenance of the authority of the classic confessional documents) and "moderns" (liberals, standing for the right, within the church, to freedom of belief and thought).

Between these two fronts stood the "ethicals," a rather diffuse group with an unclear profile, not inclined to be "modern" but also averse to the formal maintenance of confessions and juridical discipline. We have seen how Noordmans belonged to this circle from the days of his youth, granting that he had already taken a more critical position toward it by the 1920s.

Confessional Proposals: Kerkherstel and Kerkopbouw

In the summer of 1929 a formal proposal was submitted to the synod for the reorganization of the church. It was not the first of its kind, but it was unique in that it came from a commission that had been established by the synod itself. It consisted of representatives from the confessional and other orthodox groups within the Reformed Church. A prominent member of the commission was the confessional professor Th.L.Haitjema.

The commission proposed to break through the ambiguity with which the General Regulation spoke of "the doctrine" of the church and its "preservation," by expressly referring to scripture and confession. It also proposed to re-establish classical gatherings and provincial synods, as well as the General Synod, as ecclesiastical gatherings of offices, with elders as well as ministers as members—representatives "from the bottom." The General Synod would consist of representatives from all classical gatherings, as many elders as ministers. And ecclesiastical meetings must be given the ability and authority to contest decisions of "lesser" church bodies which "act against God's Word." In that way the church structure would be given not only an administrative task, but a spiritual, leading task as well. The practice of doctrinal discipline must also be enabled.

These proposals signaled a new phase in the struggle for reorganization. They became the subject of a lively discussion. Noordmans, too, involved himself in it (we shall return to that). In January 1930, an extraordinary meeting of the General Synod was held at which the proposal was rejected by the smallest majority possible (ten votes to nine). But that did not mean the end of the matter. In reaction, that same year the "Netherlands Reformed Covenant of Church Reestablishment" [*Kerkherstel*] was established on the initiative of Haitjema and his comrades. This time it was primarily the confessionals who united with other orthodox. Haitjema became the chairman. They remained passionate for a reorganization in the spirit of the 1929 proposals.

A new development emerged at the beginning of 1931, when the "Union for Church Renewal" [*Kerkopbouw*] was established alongside and in opposition to *Kerkherstel*. In this group, it was primarily ethicals and liberals who united to act for a church renewal that would include more than reorganization. Its chairman was the church professor from Utrecht (later professor of New Testament) A. M. Brouwer. Noordmans was a cofounder and became a member of the board of the *Kerkopbouw*.

As is apparent from its principles, *Kerkopbouw* emphasized the necessity of confessing the faith in the present age more than the formal maintenance of the classic confessions. Moreover it pled for ecumenical openness, for an evangelistic attitude toward outsiders, and for more emphasis on the communal nature of congregations, as well as for a greater openness to the results of academic theology. There must also be encouragement for liturgical sensibility; a church service is more than listening to a sermon! The church must also give thought to and express itself on social and international political questions, as well as be brought into close connection with the world-wide work of mission. All in all, this was a complete policy position.

Very quickly the boards of both *Kerkherstel* and *Kerkopbouw* sought contact with each other. That was difficult. A small commission for mutual consultation was indeed established; Noordmans was a member of this commission representing *Kerkopbouw*. But the board of *Kerkherstel* remained extremely critical of *Kerkopbouw*. It found that *Kerkopbouw* misunderstood the pressing necessity for reorganization. Only after reorganization had become a reality could the beautiful and wide-ranging plans of *Kerkopbouw* come to pass. Only then, that is in a churchly manner, could the question of confession properly be on the agenda. The confession, so *Kerkherstel* argued, must not be handed over to the confusing discussions of a number of arbitrary theologians; something that *Kerkopbouw* appeared not to appreciate sufficiently. That liberals shared the work of *Kerkopbouw* was another reason for *Kerkherstel* to mistrust its counterpart.

Noordmans replied on behalf of *Kerkopbouw*. In the summer of 1931 he published a short article ("Organization and Truth") in *Kerkopbouw's* new journal that expressed his reservations concerning *Kerkherstel*. His hesitance was not about the struggle for reorganization by *Kerkherstel* in itself. The circles of *Kerkopbouw* also are of the opinion, Noordmans said, that reorganization is necessary. But a distinction must be made. Roman Catholics see the institution of the church as something to be valued in itself, as holy as dogma. From the outset, Protestants could not share that vision. *Kerkherstel* appears to forget this.

> Never to my knowledge has the organization been so exclusively promoted as has now happened by prof. Haitjema *vis à vis Kerkopbouw*. The institution of the church is totally abstracted from its spiritual reality in nearly a Roman manner and is set as something of first rank beside and in opposition to the truth.[1]

Hence, Noordmans argued, the truth (the confession) is also posited as something independent in itself. Dangerous! At issue is not the organization or the truth (the confession) by themselves. Both exist in service to the proclamation and the effective work of the gospel. "The truth and the church are there for humans and not the other way around." That, said Noordmans, had brought *Kerkopbouw* into contact and collaboration with liberals. Thus

> (we) have altered nothing in the confession but we have confessed together something of the Christian truth and thereby indicated

---

[1]   *VW* 5:100.

the direction in which discussions could continue. We have done that with good conscience and no regret. Why would the Spirit of God not burn as well in that sort of discussion as in an empty, abstract organization of particular holiness?[2]

A Source of Inspiration: Gunning's
"Vertical Understanding of the Church"

The source of Noordmans's thinking concerning the course the church was taking appears in his lecture, given in the fall of 1929 at the Ethical Union, on the vision of the church held by his teacher, Gunning, a lecture that he turned into an article and published shortly thereafter. Noordmans's own passion for the church can be recognized in his sketch of Gunning's vision of the church. Noordmans in fact saw the ecclesiastical situation of his own era in the light of Gunning's vision.

He held that Gunning had not been a churchman in the ordinary sense of the word. Discussions of the church reflect a "flat" way of reasoning, Gunning maintained. Too little thought is given to the fact that the church lives from what transcends the church—its Head, Jesus Christ. What is peculiar to the church is "higher than the church." Noordmans called this Gunning's "vertical understanding of the church." However, it was not a flight into mysticism or individualism. Gunning had no desire to play the "invisible church" off against the visible (as Protestants so readily do).

> The Holy Spirit is not proud but as humble as Christ. So Gunning thinks as well of Spirit and Church. Just as the Holy Spirit can live with human failures in scripture, he is willing to do so in the church as well....Church history is in itself not yet a falling away from the Lord and the condition of the church, filled with human failure, does not hold the Spirit far from the congregation.—The sin of the church, however, is that the conditions are formalized and made legitimate; church parties are understood as self-evident and the pluriformity of the church is held as a high ideal. Gunning admonishes that to be *in* the church in the right way we have to climb up to him who is its Head, Jesus Christ.—Then the *Una Sancta* emerges in opposition to the pluriformity of the church. The parties are called to *confession*. And in the existing ruin the demand for *conversion* is heard.[3]

2 *VW* 5:100f.
3 *VW* 3:357.

To answer to that demand not only has a deeper but also a more practical effect than the confessionals' advocacy of more formal juridical discipline. The need of the church can only be overcome, not through compromise, as Gunning said, but through a "building from the ground up."

Noordmans contends that this is about a "higher practice," to be distinguished from "ordinary church politics." He sees it in his own time as a demand, and as emergent.

> The party question in our church is ever more intractable. And the pluriformity of the church in wide circles is felt not so readily as wealth any longer but often as poverty. Everything calls for the higher practice of which Gunning had been the prophet.[4]

Gunning would have nothing to do with church politics. It was about spiritual authority in the church, not the power of number, he said. Gunning saw nothing to be won with a formal reestablishment of the classical gatherings (scrapped in 1816 with the General Regulation), if it did not also mean the reestablishment of the authority of the apostles and the prophets, that is, of Holy Scripture, in the church. But he would have even less to do with a tolerance which meant in fact noncommitment: "We have no organ for revelation, so that everyone would be able to receive a higher truth. God's revelation itself wakens the organ in us. The truth brings its own light to bear." With increasing emphasis, he called for discipline in the church, but that was nothing new for him. It was consistent with his "vertical understanding of the church." That it would mean that it is sometimes necessary to come to a decision by a majority vote he reluctantly acknowledged at the end of his life.

Gunning gradually became more open to the concrete church in his conception of the church. He showed growing confidence in the spiritual authority of office-bearers/nontheologians to make judgments on things that take place in the church. As is well known, he said, what matters is not a scientific kind of knowing, but rather a "naïveté of faith." This development, this milder approach in his evaluation of people, emerged, Noordmans said, from his growing vertical thinking on the church, as he placed Christ over and against the church more to the forefront.

> More than was the case earlier, he is serious in his belief that the Holy Spirit can accompany human failures. Love waxes. His

[4]   VW 3:358.

apostles and prophets descend from their thrones; they become smaller and come closer; they come to classical gatherings.[5]

Noordmans deems this vision of the church, "with an eye to the future," still of great significance. He relates it primarily to the "mutual relation between Una Sancta and the invisible church," emphasized by Gunning. Protestants distinguish eagerly between these two, as if the visible church (the Una Sancta) would be less an article of faith than the invisible church. There is the danger of "Romanizing," where the "Una Sancta is highlighted one-sidedly from the *church-creed*." That means a "thickening" of the concept of the church. "The visibility of pope and bishops is too rough."

> The church still cannot imitate the life of heaven. It must believe it....On the other hand the seriousness, the sobriety, and simplicity of our Reformed church life may not bring us to the other extreme. The church is an object of faith and may not disappear into moral or societal life.[6]

It is good, Noordmans concluded, that Gunning, "with his strong leaning toward a Catholic church" reminds us of that!

Relativizing the Presbyterial System

With this exposition of Gunning's vision of the church, Noordmans clearly was thinking of the pending proposals for the reorganization of the church that had been introduced just a few months previously, although he does not mention them explicitly. But what he had learned from Gunning—the notion of the "higher dimension" of the church and the desire for the (also visible) catholicity of the church (the Una Sancta, the "one, holy, catholic church" as it is in the confession of faith)—he did mention in places where he engaged in direct discussion of the confessionals' proposals.

We find both elements in the article that he published in January 1930 (strategically so; it was just before the extraordinary meeting of the synod that would handle these proposals). Like Gunning in his time, he was open to the synod adopting the possibility of the practice of church discipline, but he had his reservations, reservations that had to do with his awareness of the "higher dimension" of the church. He pointed to the "eschatological character of ecclesiastical discipline" (the

---

5   *VW* 3:366.
6   *VW* 3:366.

title of his article). Church discipline is in essence a reaching into God's future. Thus, great care is demanded on this point. In his opinion, those introducing the proposal needed to be more aware of this.

Noordmans added a second, related, reservation. The old, presbyterial system (with its ecclesiastical gatherings consisting of ministers and elders/presbyters together) was desired. That elicits mixed feelings in him. It reminds him of the two streams in which the ecumenical movement had begun to manifest itself in the 1920s—"Life and Work" ("practical Christianity") and "Faith and Order" (which considered the principiel questions of church, office, and sacrament). Having established that "our church" lacks mobility, he relates that to the lack of mobility in both terrains:

> The presbyterial system is very capable...as an organization for work. It is less so as an apparatus in the work of faith and order. In that area accidents easily happen....The reorganization commission acknowledges that when it does not take an absolutely negative attitude against a more Anglican form of governance. In the management of "faith and order" an episcopal system has a wealth of wisdom, a mixture of authority and humble love which is lacking in presbyterial gatherings.[7]

If in the future doctrinal differences and disciplinary questions would be handled by a General Synod that is convened according to the presbyterial model as proposed, "I would fear that the eschatological character of church discipline would be in danger."

Here Noordmans displays his ecumenical openness, as he did in the Gunning essay when he spoke of the "Una Sancta." In that essay he had referred—in agreement—to Gunning's warning that the presbyterial system may not be "canonized." That had in fact happened, and as a consequence, Protestantism had "frozen itself half-way in a particular form." It had become a "congealed penalty." What Gunning remarked on in his time, Noordmans relates to his own: "We must return and again take up the congealed penalty, to prepare the way in humility and receptivity for the Una Sancta with its ordinances." No canonizing of the presbyterial system; this means, in fact, its relativization. Here, in his commentary on the confessional proposals for reorganization, we see how far that relativization could go for Noordmans: it brought him to a positive consideration of an Episcopal system after an Anglican model.

[7]   *VW* 5:82f.

The Proposal for Reorganization from *Kerkopbouw*

Noordmans's commentary clearly played a role in the discussions at the synod meeting in January 1930, although not necessarily a decisive one. Not only among liberals, but also among ethicals there existed considerable resistance to the confessional proposal for reorganization, with specific resistance against the plea it contained for the introduction of the practice of church discipline. Noordmans was less squarely against it. Still, the ethicals could find their real motivation for opposition articulated in Noordmans's thoughts, and in a way that many ethicals themselves were not able to put into words.

However that may be, the synod rejected the proposals, and shortly thereafter *Kerkherstel* and *Kerkopbouw* were established, two unions which both, albeit each in its own way, worked for change in the organization of the church. We saw how they came to stand not only beside each other but also in opposition to one another, and how they did not keep their mutual criticisms to themselves.

A separate proposal for reorganization was worked up by *Kerkopbouw* as a translation of its principles. It was ready in the summer of 1933. First, though, *Kerkopbouw* attempted to reach agreement with *Kerkherstel*. When that did not succeed, it published its own proposal in October 1933. Noordmans, as a member of the commission of *Kerkopbouw* that had drafted the proposal, was intimately involved. The proposal is, in fact, a concretization of his vision of the church. He had introduced the vision earlier, in the fall of 1932, while the commission was still at work, in his brochure, *Beginselen van kerkorde* [Principles of church order] (published by *Kerkopbouw*). Around the presentation of the proposal he was, as a matter of course, involved in discussions and in the church press as the principal spokesperson.

He was also the author of the official explanatory document. In it he presented the reorganization proposal from *Kerkopbouw* as on the one hand "perfectly in line with...the Haitjema Proposal" (of 1929), and on the other hand as one that differed so much that it can be characterized as "a self-standing attempt to solve the church question."

Noordmans argued that both *Kerkherstel* and *Kerkopbouw* desired a break with the existing administrative system of the Reformed Church. Both would revert to the presbyterial church order "because it is the historic one for our nation and because we deem it to be most Biblical." *Kerkopbouw's* proposal was also a plea for the reestablishment of ecclesiastical assemblies, which were to take the place of the existing administrative bodies in the church.

But this reversion to the presbyterial church order did not mean that it would simply replicate the form in which it had existed earlier in history. Following Gunning's lead, *Kerkopbouw* would take a different route.

> The...reformed system must *at least now* look different from what was proposed in the previous century. There is no church order now ready simply to be adopted....In regard to the Reformed church, we (are) now rather driven back to the command with which Jesus sent his disciples among the multitudes.[8]

So *Kerkopbouw* advocates—in the light of its time—for significant changes such that the envisioned church order could be characterized more as "*apostolic*-presbyterial."

In Its Own Time

In the light of its time. Noordmans saw his age as characterized primarily by a process of (ecclesiastical) crumbling. In the sixteenth and seventeenth centuries, church and society coincided. But, he said, we now live "in a time in which the Reformed churches often exist more in the form of a multitude than in that of a congregation." We have to take account of that. Thus the church can no longer be satisfied with the restoration of an (unchanged) organizational form from earlier centuries.

And the reality that was current for him spoke more insistently. We saw already (chapter 7) how Noordmans, speaking in May 1933 at an informational meeting of *Kerkopbouw* at Deventer, mentioned events in Russia (the church under communism) and in Germany. In Germany the movement of "German Christians," supporters of National Socialism, was afoot. (It was 1933; Adolph Hitler had just come to power.)

The persecution of the Jews, which enjoyed support from within the church in Germany, also included, he said, a political biblical criticism: "The desire is to negate the Old Testament and to purify the New." It was an attack similar to the one in a time of forced population movement, Augustine's era, when Latin Christianity was overwhelmed by the rising flood—then as well—from Russia and Germany. "The church was young then, it had survived. Will it survive now?"

The "German Christians," Noordmans had said already a year earlier in his brochure "Principles of Church Order,"

---

[8]   *VW* 5:213.

desire the "spirit of Luther" and call it "heroic piety." It is that. But in Luther they honor the German equally as much as they do the Christian....."Pure" doctrine, so beloved by Lutherans from of old, must remain so. Thus one must be prepared for war, cross, and offering. Cross and offering, that sounds very Christian, but a national tone is mixed in with it. The people of the church are at the same time a people of a race. And as with doctrine, race must remain pure. It is a piece of the order of creation and church order must take account of that....This national Christianity looks rather unlikely, as with more German matters. But it is a reality.... Moreover it exists right outside our door. Beside the order of grace proclaimed so gloriously by Luther the order of creation brutally emerges to determine the order of the church.[9]

This is the deadly danger that threatens not only the church there, but in the Netherlands as well, precisely when considering the form the church will have to take, its church order. Here too, he said, the inclination to look for a "national way of being church" exists. See the way in which "some powerful Kuyperians (cherish) a deep honor for the church of our martyrs and the heroic spirit that lived in that church." Abraham Kuyper gladly spoke in a tone of "we Calvinists." Of course Dutch Calvinists are not the same as "German Christians." "Here it is not the inspiration of race but of history. And in this, national motives work quite differently; because it is not paganism but Christianity that is its primary factor." Still, these Calvinists lay the same emphasis as the "German Christians" on the "significance of the orders of creation." Kuyper entered that plea his entire life.

One would, Noordmans said already in 1932, have to reflect before basing the church order of the future on the "orders of creation."

In the contemporary world crisis, the church must again more clearly bring to expression in its church order that it is not the *nation* but the *incarnation* that is its cornerstone, and that its only foundation is Jesus Christ. In that context, soil and history will have to step aside even more.[10]

Mobilizing an Army of Salvation

The plea for an *apostolic*-presbyterial church order is to be understood in this connection. The "apostolic" is intended as

9   *VW* 5:175f.
10   *VW* 5:178.

missionary. The Presbyterian church order old-style does in fact bind the church firmly to the soil. That can be seen in the way that congregations and classes are divided geographically, in territories. That sort of rigid division cannot be avoided completely. Still, Noordmans argued during a common meeting of *Kerkopbouw* and *Kerkherstel*,

> the church is not as strongly connected with the earth as the state. Even a national church like ours must be more mobile...the cult-congregation and with it the local congregation...remains the foundation of the church. But in a Calvinist style we also have to mobilize the church as an army of salvation.[11]

How does the proposal for reorganization from *Kerkopbouw* make this intention concrete? Firstly, through its plea concerning areas of Christian work that had been established on their own initiative outside a connection with the official church, to bring these areas under the responsibility of the church itself. This refers not only to external but also to internal mission, the latter including diaconal and ecumenical work. In his explanatory notes here, Noordmans identifies the work of the NCSV, difficult to incorporate into "old fashioned congregational life," beyond any oversight through ecclesiastical office, and yet, in content, fully ecclesiastical. It is, he said at the same common meeting, work "among the multitudes." It is not, precisely not, to take the work from the hands of those involved. No, the opposite is the case: the work itself would have to be recognized as important for the official church. Special synodical commissions would have to maintain contact with the various bodies responsible for this work. And the General Synod would have to meet periodically in an expanded arrangement with representatives of these bodies. A similar regulation would have to be put in place for classical gatherings. In that way the lay element in the church would emerge of itself.

Formation of House Churches

The proposal for reorganization made the intention to mobilize the church concrete in yet a second way: through its plea for the possibility that "house churches" be formed within local congregations, circles in which no administration of the sacraments, but certainly the proclamation of the gospel, religious education, and pastoral care could take place. Here too Noordmans comments in his explanatory notes on "the multitudes" outside (and around) the church but still not separate from it. He says of the house church,

---

[11]   *VW* 5:196.

It means an attempt to extend the congregation among the multitude, in an ecclesial way. It makes it possible for particular groups to see their desire to remain in the church satisfied without the unity of the local congregation thereby being dissolved.[12]

Those he had in mind here are minority groups with certain spiritual inclinations and groups that did not feel at home psychologically in the existing life of the congregation.

In this way, it is hoped that a step forward in the question of church parties may also be taken, so Noordmans addressed the common meeting of *Kerkopbouw* and *Kerkherstel*. Naturally,

> conflict (will) continue, for thus far it is not to be avoided. But by the extension in house churches, that conflict can be diverted and a milder climate in the church can originate. Entire groups are now embittered and sour. When they can practice spiritually under the leadership of the church, decisions will be prepared that are impossible now or that must at present result in a total splintering of the church.[13]

The initiative to form a house church, again in Noordmans's explanatory notes, could also come from the church council itself, where one envisions the reception of the estranged in the church. Hence it can be about

> groups...that are in closer touch with the most basic needs of life than the ordinary church member and who are in danger of losing their faith in the heavenly Father, and for whom it is necessary to give expression to dogma in new forms on just that point, and with a new power, so that need and doubt find a deeper echo.[14]

Or it can be about groups that "at the center of the passions of the time" experience a new "need for sanctification," by which a new confession of the Holy Spirit comes to bear. This is, par excellence, the "building of the church among the multitudes."

Required: An Episcopal Element in the Church

In his brochure, "Principles of Church Order," Noordmans had already typified the abovementioned notion of a missionary

---

12   *VW* 5:197.
13   *VW* 5:198.
14   *VW* 5:220.

("apostolic") mobilization of the church as a correction to the classic Reformed church life *downstream*, that is, "in the direction of the laity," in order to "connect with the lay movement of our time." In the same brochure he had also spoken of a necessary correction in the opposite direction: *upstream*. Calvinism, he had remarked, lacks the dimension of the historical.

> The Calvinist spirit may be deep in its consciousness of eternity and broad internationally, but it has little historical background. The rule that not only what was against scripture, but what was *not in* scripture, must fall away has freed Reformed life pretty much from traditional general Christian ways of thinking and being. More than is perhaps helpful, these churches thus display a similarity to political organizations. A republican spirit...can gain access without traditional ecclesiastical institutions and usages being able to make moderate inroads....What is peculiar to a governance by Christ finds little expression.—This danger of politicization...requires our attention. Church order may not disappear into the way of democratic parlementarianism.
>
> Upstream the Calvinist must consider that we confess an apostolic Christianity....The Reformed may not persist so strongly in their reaction that the ground of tradition sinks underfoot. Jesus has not only sent the Holy Spirit, but he has also given tasks to some humans....When this notion is completely lost, the discernment of the spirits is replaced by the counting of noses. It cannot be said how much power is thereby lost in the church.[15]

In this context Noordmans had, as in his article, "The Eschatological Character of Church Discipline," in 1930, pointed to the Anglican Church. That church had maintained the concept of history in a better way.

> We are frightened to the bone of hierarchy and we have reasons for that. But we are in danger of throwing out the baby with the bathwater....We do not need to take over the episcopate from the Anglicans....But...there is just enough there for us to take something of its advantage. By cutting off the old Christian past so completely...we have kept too little of the true episcopal *spirit* in the offices....It must be possible to graft something of this wood onto the stem of the "classic Reformed life."[16]

[15]   *VW* 5:180f.
[16]   *VW* 5:181f.

In these considerations we come upon the word "apostolic" for a second time. Apparently, with Noordmans that word does not only mean "missionary"—directed to the multitudes—but also "episcopal"—directed to history, tradition. The apostolicity for which Noordmans pleas includes for him both necessary corrections of "the classic Reformed church life," upstream and downstream, together. "The one hand grips Christ, the 'Shepherd and Guardian of (our) souls' (1 Peter 2:25). The other grips sinners, the true laity." Both movements, apparently contradictory, are in reality together an "indication of the essence of the church."

Discipline—Not Political but Episcopal-Pastoral

Noordmans had argued in his 1932 brochure (as in his article of 1930) that an episcopal element in the church would be of great importance to the practice of church discipline as well. It was only that this element may not be drawn into a political atmosphere. For this, it is necessary to appoint people "for a longer duration and with a greater view to personal qualities." The Reformed Church was already acquainted with that sort of role in the figure of the visitor.[17] But he had no more than administrative authority. "This institution could perhaps be constructed in this direction," in the direction of a pastoral episcopate as practiced by someone like Augustine.

The reorganization proposal from *Kerkopbouw* presented such an attempt. It was proposed that besides the offices of minister, elder, and deacon, the function of visitor would be instituted, which would be filled in each province by a minister and at the national level by a minister with the title of "moderator," to be named by the General Synod. The visitors and moderator would be appointed for a term of six years and have as their task the oversight of office-bearers, that they "fulfill their calling in agreement with the essence and the historic confession of the Church." The visitors do not receive a new (let alone a "higher") office in this proposal. Still, in the appearance of the visitors, as proposed, something of the episcopal/personal exists. So it was in fact intended. If intervention was necessary in particular cases, then, writes Noordmans in an explanatory article in October 1933, the new institution of church visitation could, it was hoped, serve to "temper the passion and the animosity of the presbyterial process of discipline through an episcopal spirit."

---

[17]   [Tran. The "visitor" is a figure that has appeared in church orders of the past. It is not an office. It is a new role/function being proposed.]

CHAPTER 10

Continuing Controversy over Church Renewal

Criticism of *Kerkopbouw*'s Reorganization Proposal

In the mid-1930s, Noordmans found himself in the middle of the developments in the national church. As one the principal authors of *Kerkopbouw*'s reorganization proposal, he was fully involved in interpreting and defending it. Published in October 1933, it was on the agenda of the General Synod at its meeting in the summer of 1934. However, the synod postponed substantive discussion to a special meeting of the synod in January 1935. Preceding the synod's discussions, there were lively interchanges in the church press. Criticism came most specifically from *Kerkherstel* with its chair, Haitjema, as its most important spokesperson.

The *Kerkherstel* criticism was not directed against the entire proposal. There was agreement with the proposal to break with the existing administrative system of the Reformed Church and to return to a presbyterial church order that would include the re-establishment of ecclesiastical assemblies as well as the possibility of the practice of church discipline (which had already been in the confessional proposals of 1929). There was further agreement with the proposal to incorporate a number of Christian activities into the church that thus far had been unconnected with the official church.

But the reaction was expressly negative regarding the proposals for the formation of house churches and the institution of a new style of visitation. Those were deemed to be in conflict with the "desire to return to a presbyterial church order."As to the formation of house churches, this approach to an "apostolic" ecclesiastical flexibility went too far for *Kerkherstel*. It was thought that the formation of house churches as proposed would shatter the unity of the local congregation, that party strife within the church would be provoked rather than softened, and that the existing, sinful division of the church would be put in the regulations and thereby sanctioned. And as to the regulation on visitation, *Kerkherstel* saw this as a tendency toward the creation of a new office, specifically the visitor-moderator, one that would be elevated beyond the other offices of the church, not serving but ruling, a sort of "Roman bishop." That would conflict with presbyterial order and would be unacceptable per definition.

Kerkherstel's criticism raised still another point: the proposed addition to the envisioned new General Regulations of two introductory articles on the essence, goal, and task of the Netherlands Reformed Church. The church, as it was formulated there, is "part of the One General Christian Church, built on Jesus Christ as its only foundation."And it "has as its goal the proclamation of the Word of God in connection with its historic confession." That includes as its tasks, among other things, "care for the confession in order that the faith of the church in its symbolic and liturgical documents" (i.e., in its confessional writings and formularies for worship) "comes ever more purely to expression"; the internal and external mission; the maintenance of contacts "with other parts of the One General Christian Church"; and the witness to God's commands in "the life of the individual and society."

The reservation against this fundamental (and ecumenical) opening was that it sounded like a (new) confession. A church order, so reasoned *Kerkherstel*, is not itself a "confession"; it can and may only point to the existing, historic confessions. To do more here gives at least the appearance of the formulation of a new confession, thereby robbing the classic confession of its (exclusive) authority. Indeed, "care for the confession," denoted as an ecclesiastical task, also evoked anxiety. That uneasiness was primarily concerned with the statement that the aim would be that the "faith of the church" might "come ever more purely to expression" in its official documents. Would the proponents then alter the authority of the existing confessional documents? For *Kerkherstel* the reorganization of the church would always have to consist of a return of the church to its historic confession and, in the end, would preserve it (if need be through discipline).

"We have entered open sea with the church"

In the spring of 1934, Noordmans published his brochure, *Evangelie en volkskerk* [Gospel and the people's church]. In it he responded to the final reservation noted above. He again noted the current situation—events in Germany. He sharply criticized what he called the backwards-looking attitude of *Kerkherstel*. They appeared to desire the exclusive reintroduction of an earlier shape of the church. They would also preserve as closely as possible the old, well-known confession by familiar means. But, he argued, new questions have arisen! We no longer have to do with questions from the nineteenth century:

> We are so forcefully thrown back on the biblical contradictions between Baal or the Lord, nature or the Creator, that abstract scientific, natural paganism thereby appears to be an innocent by-product....Such awful things are happening, the breakers are so high, that we get the feeling, or more correctly feel the belief growing within us, that the church is now more itself than in quieter times....We no longer sail in the water where one must be alert for any ripple because a dangerous reef may be hidden beneath the surface. We have entered open sea with the church. It will be hard enough to keep the boat steady, but it has water before the bow and one need not look anxiously if the depth finder indicates five, six, or seven feet. One does not make or evaluate church regulations in view of little dodges or tricks....It is about God's Spirit and the main point of the gospel....We are beyond the time of academic discipline and have entered the time of the discipline of the nations, and in that storm all the subtleties of an academic sort will be blown away....It is not paganism at the margin, that of the academic, but paganism in our midst, paganism among the populace, that demands our thought.[1]

It is this situation, Noordmans argued, that *Kerkopbouw* reckons with in its proposal for reorganization. That is why those two introductory fundamental articles are so important.

---

[1]   VW 5:283, 285f.

"The Netherlands Reformed Church, as part of the one General Christian Church"; so it is not a national but a catholic church. "Built on Jesus Christ as its only foundation"; consequently not on soul, race, or blood. "Has as its goal the proclamation of the Word of God in connection with its historic confession"; therewith the Christian confession is maintained, with the inclusion of the Old Testament.[2]

How suspicious *Kerkherstel* still was! Noordmans went on: "With the church's past behind us and Christ above us we need...not be anxious." In any case, we must not fixate on the "existing 'contradictions' within the ever-shrinking multitude which still belongs to the church." If we do that we "slowly but surely run aground." No, "the church has to engage the debate that is taking place in the *great* multitude outside the church door." Certainly, we cannot do without the historic confession. It comes down "to the purity of the message...but with that not everything is said. We cannot preach in a vacuum." Hence the new accents in the proposal: the apostolic and the episcopal.

Rejection and a New Start

Kerkopbouw's proposal never had a chance. Like the confessionals' proposals of 1929, it was rejected. Its opponents came as much from the "left" (liberals who would have nothing to do with discipline) as from the "right" (confessionals who judged that the proposal was unclear on the preservation of the confession). Noordmans's principled plea had been unable to convince the opponents.

Not unexpectedly, the synod's decision evoked great regret among the members of *Kerkopbouw*. One week later, the executive committee of *Kerkopbouw* met in an atmosphere of crisis, for more than one reason. Noordmans was not present; he had mentioned why in a short letter. For him the synod meeting that had just concluded had provided another reason for regret. A new church professor for Utrecht was appointed at the meeting. Noordmans had stood as a candidate, but, again, he was not appointed (see chapter 7). Still harder for him was the fact that Brouwer, for many years Noordmans's friend and comrade in *Kerkopbouw* and, in his capacity as church professor from Utrecht, functioning as a synod advisor, had advised the synod against Noordmans. Brouwer had been frank with Noordmans previously on that account, but that did not sweeten the pill for Noordmans. He had

---

[2]   *VW* 5:284.

written bitterly (in a letter to K.H. Miskotte): "While the Reorganization Proposal—for which I had written the outline, the elucidation of principles, and the apology—lay on the table at the synod, Brouwer had supposedly declared that I was too old to teach dogmatics and church order." Noordmans could not bring himself, under these conditions, to attend the meeting with Brouwer as chair, while Brouwer, apparently unhappy with the way things had turned out, placed his chairmanship on the table as a matter of discussion. There were even discussions of whether *Kerkopbouw* itself should be disbanded.

But it was decided to continue under Brouwer's chairmanship and to continue to work for reorganization. The commission that had proposed *Kerkopbouw*'s plan remained; continuing attentiveness and activity were deemed necessary.

It was also decided to seek further contact with *Kerkherstel*. The administrators of *Kerkherstel* appeared also to desire further contact. It was thought from both sides that a new, third attempt at reorganization would only have a chance of succeeding if the two groups joined forces.

"Common search in the direction of our object"

Following a short absence, Noordmans resumed his collaboration. Again he threw his theological weight on the scale to help overcome hesitance to work further on reorganization and to help prepare spirits in broader circles for a *rapprochement* between *Kerkopbouw* and *Kerkherstel*. In June 1935, he spoke to a general meeting of members of *Kerkopbouw* on "the immediate future of the church." He rejected the notion that it would all come down "to the Holy Spirit" and, thus, a planned reorganization of the church would not be necessary. "No. Spirit and organization do not exclude but include each other....We squander the Spirit with a defective organization."

In this connection, Noordmans criticized the conservatism not only of the synod but also of the various ecclesiastical parties. The church now stands with the world in a crisis, he said, such that we can no longer be satisfied with worn-out clichés. Old divisions fall away. We must now be "positively biblical."

The liberals should allow themselves to be addressed in this way, he continued. They prefer to approach faith scientifically. Faith in Christ gives them every reason to take that option. They then raise the question about the "historical Jesus." But in our days Christ is seen more in connection with God the Father and with the Holy Spirit. Now it is just faith in God the Father and the Spirit that is under attack. A scientific approach has less of a handle on that.

The ethicals should also allow themselves to be addressed in this way. They gladly flirt with culture and have their sights set on higher, culturally sophisticated circles. But in so doing they do not understand that the gospel is intended for all people, of all ranks and classes.

It is about confession. Science and culture cannot lead the church:

> We are driven back to the confession....The church will have to be and remain the church, itself. We confess; there everything is said....Will we all have to become confessional? Why not? What will the church do other than confess? But it is not an everyday, peaceful work. No eating up of our own capital. No living off past investments. The church will be hard put against the gods of this age. It will have to make its confession among the multitudes.... The confession is not a recording.[3] Hence it is necessary that we have an organization. But don't we have one?....We do. But in today's rough world the church has to adjust to reality....The organization of 1816 was not well-made. It had no handles. We must continue a common search in pursuit of our proposal.[4]

The Accord, Progress toward a New Proposal for Reorganization

By means of this powerful argument, Noordmans helped his comrades in *Kerkopbouw* overcome their hesitations, and he instilled in *Kerkherstel* greater confidence in the possibility of common action. His plea for a new kind of confession in the face of new challenges showed that he did not simply allow himself to be drawn into *Kerkherstel*'s orbit. At the same time his plea for a "positively biblical" institution and his assertion that confessing[5] is at issue were well accepted by *Kerkherstel*.

Indeed, it appeared that the differences between *Kerkherstel* and *Kerkopbouw* were no longer unbridgeable. An agreement was reached already in September 1935, and together they requested that the synod place reorganization on the agenda again as quickly as possible. The synodical administration (the General Synod Commission) appointed a number of its members as observers to continuing discussions of a common commission of representatives of *Kerkopbouw* (among them Noordmans) and *Kerkherstel*. In the winter of 1935-36, this commission

---

3   [Trans. Dutch *grammofoonplaat*, one is to imagine the old vinyl records.]

4   *VW* 5:320f.

5   [Trans. In Dutch a distinction is made between *belijden*—"confess" as a verb— and *belijdenis*—"confession" as a noun. This distinction was maintained by the Netherlands Reformed Church throughout its official documents. When the church confesses, it is an action, not simply adherence to a document.]

worked the agreement that had been achieved into a formal accord. It had the form of a number of amendments to *Kerkopbouw*'s proposal. These were concessions to *Kerkherstel* that, in the opinion of *Kerkopbouw*, did not affect the essential elements of the original proposal.

It had been agreed to replace the two introductory articles on the essence and goal of the church with a formulation (to be added later in the document) that recalled the "historic confessional documents and liturgical formularies." The representatives of *Kerkopbouw* were sensitive to the reservation that their original proposal had evoked the appearance of an intention to introduce a new confession. Moreover, besides dealing with "the care for the confession," the document now also spoke of its "preservation." That too was a concession to *Kerkherstel*. On the other hand, the representatives of *Kerkherstel* had accepted the understanding that care for the confession also includes giving the faith an "ever purer expression."

There was further agreement to replace the proposed regulation for the possibility of house churches with a number of articles that gave the church council greater and more specific authority to form groups and categories. These articles were amplified with a number of transitional regulations for organizations of church members who wished to remain free of ecclesiastical connection. That way the existence of party differences in the church was acknowledged (as *Kerkopbouw* had advocated). On the other side, it was hoped that giving these regulations a transitional character would avoid what *Kerkherstel* feared: that the existing "sinful division" would be sanctioned through official rules. Transitional regulations always govern emergency situations, not a normal situation.

The proposal concerning the function of the visitor/moderator was retained. Representatives of *Kerkherstel* recognized the importance of a more personal element in oversight and discipline. However, it was now emphatically determined that the visitors and the moderator would have only an advisory voice in the provincial and General synods and that in addition to ministers, elders could be appointed as visitors or moderators. Both amendments were intended to remove *Kerkherstel*'s fear of a concealed importation of the office of bishop.

A Phenomenon

The Accord agreed upon in the commission received approval from the boards of *Kerkopbouw* and *Kerkherstel*. That appears more remarkable than it was, as the organizations had moved closer to each other.

Kerkherstel had in the years following 1930 gained a greater understanding of the need to be open to the great questions of the time that, in turn, made a new confession urgent. *Kerkopbouw*, for its part, had consented to an adjustment of its earlier proposal towards a greater consideration of the (confessing) unity of the church, with somewhat less room for division in the church and with more openness to the eventual necessity of the practice of discipline. It had already spoken—carefully—of discipline in its own reorganization proposal, albeit in variance to its original set of principles, in which *Kerkopbouw* had expressly spoken against the preservation of ecclesiastical order through the "disciplinary process."

Still, the fact that the Accord happened at all had great significance. The differences between *Kerkherstel* and *Kerkopbouw* were not separate from the existing party conflicts. Here—for the first time in the history of the Reformed Church—the rigid status quo of parties was broken through in a manner that could mean a way out of the impasse in the church.

That this was possible was in large part due to Noordmans. It is true that he had clearly in 1930, in opposition to the then pending proposals of *Kerkherstel*, pointed to the "eschatological character of ecclesiastical discipline." But earlier, in his lecture on Gunning's view of the church, he had (implicitly) spoken against noncommitted tolerance in the church and thus for the practice of discipline (chapter 9 above). We saw him, following the rejection of *Kerkopbouw's* proposal, plead for the continuation of the struggle for reorganization in such a way that greater appreciation could grow in the circles of *Kerkopbouw* for the concerns and intentions of *Kerkherstel*, and so that at the same time confidence could grow in the circles of *Kerkherstel* for the aspirations of *Kerkopbouw*.

The Accord was offered as a joint result to the General Synod. It was accepted in the synod's meeting of August 1936 as a starting point for a newly drafted proposal for reorganization. The commission that had worked out the Accord was given the task of working on this new proposal for reorganization. The commission was expanded with a number of representatives from other sectors of the church (including the Reformed League). The Accord itself was published in the fall of 1936. The new proposal would be ready in the summer of 1937 and subsequently presented directly to the General Synod, which would discuss it in a special meeting in January 1938.

Questions in Church Order Are Questions of Faith

Naturally, public discussions took place in the run up to January 1938. Noordmans, a member of the commission that had drafted the Accord and worked on the new proposal, spoke at the ministers meeting of 1937 on the theme, "Church Order." He emphasized the substantial weight of this (apparently dry) theme. Church order is not only a matter of practical organization. There are questions of principle, questions of faith at issue. It is a misunderstanding to play Spirit and order off against each other, as if the Holy Spirit has to do only with charismata, "gifts of the Spirit," and not also with ecclesiastical offices!

It was not for nothing that the Reformers had pushed through a reformation in church order—and there more radically than in doctrine. Luther had, in his book-burning at Wittenberg, thrown the entire (Roman Catholic) canon law into the fire! He himself did not subsequently draw up his own church order but rather left organizational questions to the governing authority. For him the only important thing was that the gospel would be proclaimed, and thus there would be a preaching office. But he left the preacher unprotected, all alone, out in the cold. Calvin, however, did develop a church order, with an elaborated structure of offices—minister, elder, and deacon (and also, at first, doctor, as teacher, interpreter of the Bible, although the function of the office of doctor remained in doubt). For this he went back to the Bible and the early church—not as an exegetical-historical researcher of "how it had been earlier," but in faith:

> Luther did not dare construct a full wife, a valiant bride of Christ, from the rib of the office of minister. When Calvin participated in Lutheran church life in his Strasburg years, he was moved with compassion with the position of the Lutheran preachers, as they did their work unprotected from every side....He instituted four offices, and in so doing returned to the authority of scripture in full spiritual sense, as one having authority.[6]

It comes down to that appeal to scripture today, said Noordmans. Thus we have to do with Catholicism as the great opponent, one not to be underestimated, and in particular with the modern, more mystically oriented Catholicism. That too goes back to the Bible and the old church. As such it ends up with the bishop. Calvin omitted the bishop and ended up with the presbyter (in the Reformed tradition one began

---

[6]   *VW* 5:372.

to distinguish between the "teaching" presbyter, the preacher, and the "ruling" presbyter, the elder.)

Behind this difference there is a difference in the concept of church, as Noordmans pointed out. Is the church a sacramental reality, the "body of Christ," the continuation of the incarnation, or even Christ himself? Or is it a spiritual reality in which Christ works through Word and Spirit? The first conception is that of Catholicism; the second that of (Reformed) Protestantism. With the first conception the vision of office as an *organ of the church* applies, in the liturgy, in service of a continuing stream of grace via the sacraments; the office itself then serves as the peculiar glory of the church. With the second conception the offices are *instruments of God*.

> The space in which they work is not a visible body. Life is not the category from which they must be understood, but faith....The offices are free; they are turned outward and the church, which they have to serve, is not an enclosed unity, not an organic body, not organic life, not a liturgically harmonic movement or dance, but the kingdom of Christ must be established in the spaces of heaven and earth, time and eternity, the open world of God: the church under the stars.[7]

Here the Word precedes. This too is catholicity, but differently so. "Reformed religion is Catholicism that goes back from the pope to Peter."

Confrontation with Catholicism: Elder versus Bishop

It is remarkable in this lecture that Noordmans emphatically signals a contradiction between bishop and presbyter (elder). We find here nothing of his earlier openness to the figure of the bishop and the consequent relativization of the presbyterial system. Likewise, his earlier expressed positive attitude to Anglicanism no longer appears. Apparently a shift had taken place in Noordmans's position. More than before, he was convinced of the importance of Calvin's insights into church order and the tradition of Reformed church order.

That appears still more clearly in his discussion at that same time (between April and November 1937) with Brouwer. He (chair of *Kerkopbouw*, since 1935 professor of New Testament at Utrecht), had argued in his book, *De kerkorganistie der eerste eeuw en wij* [The organization

[7]   *VW* 5:372f.

of the church of the first century and we] (published at the beginning of 1937), that no one particular model of the church can be derived from the New Testament to be used as a measure, and that thus no ecclesiastical tradition can claim that its organization is especially the "demand of God's Word," not even the Reformed tradition. According to Brouwer, only practical arguments measured against a goal can be determinative for the structure and organization of the church.

In the lecture cited above, Noordmans noted that position. But he felt compelled, in opposition to Brouwer, to return expressly to argue a biblical basis for the presbyterial system. He did so in a series of articles in *Kerkopbouw's* newspaper.

Noordmans believed that he had to respond to Brouwer's book particularly in the matter of the controversy with Rome. In his lecture he had mentioned the nineteenth-century (originally Anglican but later) Roman Catholic theologian, Cardinal J. H. Newman, who had struck a more spiritual, mystical, tone in his thinking on the church. He had learned of Newman's thought in a dissertation on it (published in 1936) by W. H. van de Pol, himself involved with *Kerkopbouw* (and who later, like Newman, would become Roman Catholic). Newman's thought, as represented by Van de Pol, had impressed Noordmans. It was his conviction that Newman's vision, which had inspired modern Catholic theologians with a vision of the church, could become dangerously attractive to (Reformed) Protestants. They should not forget that a principal difference between Rome and the Reformation (in the understanding of the church and the doctrine of grace) was in the balance! He had already sounded a note of warning in his lecture: "We must not underestimate the power of Catholic thought." In his reaction to Brouwer's argument, Noordmans underlined this warning.

> Reformed churches are built on scripture and when we still feel the peculiar bonds in our spiritual, Protestant life, we cannot let go of that. As soon as that faith in what we are about is lacking with us, and we already no longer believe that it is God's business, then the tradition, as Rome confesses it, comes upon us as iron shackles of necessity that imprison us. It is not an accident that Newman is now in vogue. It is not a small thing when this athlete of the spirit comes upon you. Whoever has read Van de Pol's dissertation looks about to see whether there might be some help against this threatening, rising power. [8]

---

[8]   *VW* 5:392.

It will not suffice for us, Noordmans claims, to appeal on behalf of our system to purely practical goals. Whoever deprives himself, through Brouwer's exegetical-historical argument, of every possibility of appeal to the Bible, has in fact already capitulated to Rome. Rome certainly appeals to the Bible and will continue to do so all the more as we abandon the attempt. Rome believes in what it is about. When we have no faith in what we are about, then we are losers in the confrontation.

So appeal to the Bible is necessary as a matter of faith. In that appeal you cannot remain at the level of the literary-historical. It is more a matter of hearing the entire biblical witness, of "drawing on scripture through the Spirit and with power," in order that a new future can open for the church. That is what Calvin did when he highlighted the presbyter and so really (as opposed to both Luther and the Baptists) created a church order.

> The commentaries of Calvin have a two-fold significance. An *academic* one—and then they can be compared with those by scholars from all ages. The Reformer will then have to give way on some points....But the *world-historical* value of his biblical interpretation is something else. Then he is less easy to refute, for in that case the Bible interprets itself and God has his hand in.[9]

At present one cannot simply institute new offices as one pleases. Brouwer had proposed the consideration of church professors of the Netherlands Reformed Church (who since the educational law of 1876 had functioned in the national universities) as modern representatives of the office of "doctor" (which had surfaced with Calvin but had since disappeared). Noordmans deemed this a misunderstanding. A new discovery like that cannot simply—again on the basis of practical considerations—be posited as an office.

> There must be a higher necessity buried within it. An office is an ecclesiastical form, derived from the Bible, in which something of the power of creation resides. When Calvin moved the pawn of the elder on the chessboard, he thereby checkmated the pope. I cannot see that Brouwer's suggestion meets such conditions. Why precisely these functionaries, who have gotten half lost outside the theological faculty and therefore are now assisting in the church, would be indicated as a reincarnation of the old-Christian teacher or the Calvinist doctor is not clear to me.[10]

---

[9]   *VW* 5:395.
[10]   *VW* 5:396.

An office of the church is something other than a ministry of the church. There are many ministries. Others can also emerge according to the fields of work which appear to be areas of work for the church. But

> the office always possesses particular characteristics that cannot be explained from service alone....There is something mystical to it—the Una Sancta speaks in it; the beginning and the ending present themselves; original Christianity and the church of the end (eschaton), the heavenly church. There is a structure of the body of Christ which is mystically given in the scripture and which speaks the last word in the world-historical debate.[11]

Thus not every ministry can simply be seen as an office. The elder is certainly, but not, for example, the ministry of visitation. That ministry, however important it is for the procedure of church discipline, must not be seen as an office. Were that to happen, "then it would share in the mystic nature of the church and over time one could not distinguish it from the episcopate. The hierarchy then makes its entrance."

So Noordmans here distanced himself emphatically from the figure of the bishop, even in connection with the function of the church visitor. In 1932, in his *Principles of Church Order*, he had advocated for the element of the "episcopal" in this connection. He was still in favor of that element. But more sharply than at that time, he now rejected the notion of hierarchy in the church. Then he had said that that when one resists this, one must be careful not to throw out the baby with the bathwater. Now Noordmans no longer fostered that consideration. Without reserve he had in the meantime gotten behind Reformed, presebyterial church order as the only valid alternative to a Catholic, episcopal model, one that appeared to him very threatening.

Last Attempt at Interpretation

In January 1938, the synod discussed the new reorganization proposal, the provisions that executed the Accord. In the meantime, great differences of opinion within *Kerkopbouw* had emerged. Many, Brouwer among them, had serious reservations concerning the process of discipline as it was set out as a possibility in the proposal. Still, the proposal had broader support than the earlier ones of 1930 and 1935. Unlike those, this was accepted in its first reading (again by the minimum majority, ten votes to nine). It would be discussed in the

[11]   *VW* 5:398.

classical meetings and the provincial administrations in their May and June meetings.

In the first half of 1938 public discussions grew intense. There were protests from both the Reformed League and from the liberals. Signs of what could be expected as reactions from the classical and provincial meetings did not appear positive. That gave Noordmans an occasion in the late spring to wage a last attempt to avoid a shipwreck at this late stage. Once again, in his brochure *Kerkelijk denken voorwaarde voor kerkorde* [Thinking ecclesiastically: a condition for church order], he sketched the pressing need for reorganization. A confession cannot function in an unbiblical, secular organization of the church, he argued. It is no wonder that a "new church front" had been forming for decades. Mission, the ecumenical movement, and the liturgical movement (which is about the essence of worship) all press in the direction of a more ecclesiastical understanding. The church struggle in Germany, where men like the Reverend Martin Niemöller have to bear imprisonment, shows how this need is present there and is an encouragement for the church in the Netherlands.

> The confessing movement in Germany appears to be a weak attempt of a church to maintain itself....It is developed under the cross; it proceeds simply by the way of obedience; it is centered in the proclamation of the gospel, and it demonstrates to us the frontiers of the civic. This...manifests to many in our age, who were prepared in reference to the church to pass to the order of the day, the significance of the church yet again. Many, whose feet had nearly slipped (Ps. 73:2) felt something of the ground, on which all this rests again. The Rev. Niemöller's imprisonment, a piece of "ordinary" pastoral history, does more than a gigantic house party.[12]

It is with this "new church front," argued Noordmans, that the reorganization proposal coheres. He sketched once again its outlines, emphasizing that the entire piece follows the lines of the one earlier proposed be *Kerkopbouw*. It adheres closely to a presbyterial church order. Or better stated, it re-establishes it, for it makes the administrative bodies (with elders as administrators/representatives of the people and ministers as bureaucrats) into assemblies (with elders and ministers as office-bearers all) of the church once again. But it also

---

[12]   *VW* 5:441f.

enlarges this presbyterial church order through further regulations concerning oversight and discipline (the confession must be preserved as a principle of church order) and through the establishment (with an eye on the need of the age) of new ministries for a variety of work that could have no place under the administrative regime, ministries like mission and contact with those estranged from the church (internal mission). *Kerkopbouw's* earlier proposal had that last ministry in mind with its notion of house churches; that idea had now been changed to the idea that in every (large) congregation, a contact commission for this work must be formed.

Noordmans considered separately those points that were being so hotly contested: confession and discipline. He sharply refuted the liberal criticism that would (*nota bene*, with an appeal to the gospel!) know nothing of the relationship between church order and confession. If this relationship falls away, then only regulations are left, not a church order. Indeed, with the description of the essence and goal of the church, the confessional writings are noted in the proposal, for they give explanatory descriptions with the "pictures" of various church tasks; they give understanding to what is meant by gospel, sacrament, mission. There is no reason to be anxious about that sort of reference:

> Mature people...always ask what the confessional writings are doing in the church order. They ask whether that is not a "stick behind the door" and whether they are not too old for it to be used. I repeat, that they...are not intended to be a *stick* to strike, but a *staff* to guide.[13]

Discipline, of which this speaks, is not intended in a regulative sense, as if it was the intention to place ecclesiastical halters around each other's necks or eventually to catch people in their words. Indeed, it concerns not only the preaching of this or that minister, but the entirety of all church tasks. As envisioned, it would be practiced in an ecclesiastical manner, not through articles, but by humans; likewise, the institution of church visitors for the practice of an oversight that precedes discipline.

The word *episcopal*, a word that Noordmans still had used in his discussion with Brouwer in connection with the work of the visitors, no longer flowed from his pen. His ecumenical openness had remained, but more decisively than before his orientation was turned to the presbyterial church order of the Reformed tradition.

---

[13]   *VW* 5:458.

Failure Yet Again

Noordmans's brochure was the occasion for Brouwer to declare himself "totally against the proposal." He did not at all appreciate Noordmans's careful argument concerning confession and discipline. What he saw in it convinced him that the proposal came down to a confirmation of the old, static notion of the church and an adherence to the classic confessional writings without a real openness for a new beginning. That was absolutely unacceptable to him.

More of Brouwer's colleagues in *Kerkopbouw* distanced themselves from the proposal in the course of the discussions. They viewed cooperation with *Kerkherstel*, which had led to the recent proposal, with anxiety. One of them was Brouwer's colleague at Utrecht, H. Th. Obbink, professor of religious history and Old Testament. He was the chief editor of the *Algemeen Weekblad voor Christendom en Cultuur*, for a long time the primary organ of the Ethical Party but more and more the mouthpiece for those in *Kerkopbouw* who evidenced reservations (the "left wing"). In a letter to Noordmans, he gave voice to his own reservations. "Are these really the days to return to Dort? The spirit that speaks from the *Kerkherstellers* frightens me. And that '*Kerkopbouwers*' go along in making the church a dogmatic regulated unity! Poor Reformed Church. You can no longer return. I certainly see that. And you can never win me for your fruitless battle....You belong to *Kerkherstel*. *Kerkopbouw* has been lured into the trap, innocently!" A short time later Noordmans's name was quietly removed from the list of coworkers on the *Algemeen Weekblad*. There, apparently, his contributions were no longer welcome.

More and more, Noordmans came to stand alone within *Kerkopbouw*—perhaps precisely because he came closer to sharing the convictions of *Kerkherstel*. In the same way, his theological development had brought him into an ever clearer independent position *vis à vis* the Ethical Party from which he had come.

In May 1938, throughout the entire nation, provincial administrations held their gatherings; in June the classical gatherings met. The majority of the church meetings as a whole, as well as of the voting members (counted together), appeared to be against the proposal. The General Synod, in August 1938, did little more than to state that the proposal that had been accepted provisionally in January 1938 apparently had failed to reach the required agreement. The matter was referred to the General Synod commission (the synod administration) and was again on the agenda on August 8, 1939. There were proposals to start reorganization yet again, but they were all rejected. The case for reorganization and church renewal appeared definitely to have come to a dead end.

Noordmans had yet again fought a futile battle. Still, the matter was not really off track. Less than a month after the latest decision of the synod, the Second World War broke out. Netherlands would be caught up in the violence of war. The German occupation would bring completely new conditions to bear. Therein would lie a new possibility where the "possibilities" of the previous ten years had failed. And Noordmans's role would not have been exhausted.

In the meantime, he saw further cooperation with *Kerkopbouw* as doing little good. At the end of 1939, he resigned his membership.

CHAPTER 11

Liturgy

The Liturgical Movement

Despite the synodical decisions of 1938 and 1939, Noordmans must have been convinced that the reorganization of the church was not a dead issue. Not for nothing had he emphasized (in "Thinking Ecclesiastically: A Condition for Church Order," Spring 1938) that a "new front" had formed in the church—already decades in the making and in the face of all the opposing official factors—of powers intent on overcoming the secularized state of the church. The rejection of all the proposals for reorganization in August 1939 had not been able to alter the existence of this "front."

Noordmans had specifically named the Liturgical Movement as one of the factors in renewal. It had officially begun shortly after 1920, when the "Liturgical Circle" was established by a number of pioneers. It was a study circle of (primarily) ministers belonging to the Ethical Party. A series of liturgical handbooks had been published, followed in 1934 by a more extensive *Handboek voor de Eredienst* [Handbook for worship]. In 1935, the circle had taken the initiative of establishing a

Liturgical Union, which was open for membership for all who were interested. A yearly liturgical conference was organized.

A central figure in the movement was G. van der Leeuw, chair of both the circle and the union. He and many of his comrades in the Liturgical Movement also belonged to *Kerkopbouw*. Van der Leeuw was a leading figure there as well. It was no surprise that the ideas of the Liturgical Movement enjoyed a broad hearing in *Kerkopbouw* (although they were not universally shared). We saw already (chapter 9) that *Kerkopbouw* had the encouragement of a liturgical sensibility as one of its policy proposals. *Kerkopbouw* had constituted a special commission in this area (with Van der Leeuw as one of its members). This commission had published its own report in 1933, *Het wezen van den Eredienst* [The Essence of Worship].

In his brochure of the Spring of 1938, Noordmans had spoken approvingly of this "work on the liturgy":

> It emerges from a powerful notion of new life in the church and a new love for ecclesiastical forms; for a *church order* in the broadest sense....The Liturgical Movement...brings many young people, in particular, who for a long time found themselves more at home in the open air, back within the walls of the church. And it teaches them to worship in forms that are responsible to scripture and the confession. Secular forms in particular are an atrocity for the modern liturgist.[1]

Critical Remarks

Noordmans had given voice to a number of reservations he had concerning the work being done in pursuit of a new liturgy. The Liturgical Movement could go in a variety of directions, and Noordmans was not indifferent as to which direction it would go. But besides certain undesirable tendencies, he clearly saw positive possibilities. As he wrote, it is

> Absolutely not certain, and not even likely that rich and luxurious forms will be the result. The Liturgical Movement can, following an understandable catholicizing expansion, just as well return to extremely simple forms, in agreement with Reformed religion.[2]

He had also shown earlier that he had carefully followed the Liturgical Movement with interest. That was in 1935, in a discussion of

[1]   *VW* 5:441.
[2]   *VW* 5:441.

the book, *De incarnatie* [The incarnation], by the Groningen professor (and ethical theologian) W. J. Aalders. In it, Noordmans had expressed himself critically on the manner in which the book had viewed "the mystery of the incarnation" as an active principle of the connection of God and the human, particularly in the church, and so as an intensification of the creation. That this book also cited the Liturgical Movement as involved in this sort of incarnational thought had drawn from Noordmans a few critical remarks of the same sort. In his view, this kind of incarnational thinking "leaves no full place" for preaching, and so for the peculiar work of the Spirit.

> Aalders's conception is for me finally too academic, too philosophical. He works too much with "being" and too little with the Word. Being is mysterious; the Word is sharply dividing. Behind the latter stands preaching, and behind that the Holy Spirit. The continuing nature of the incarnation may not put the Holy Spirit in the shadow. I am of the opinion that this happens too often in Aalders's book.[3]

Thus, alertness is demanded in relation to the Liturgical Movement!

Noordmans had given his discussion of Aalders's book the title, "Mystery or Message." Is the church an experience of mystery or is it about hearing the message? In what was for him an unavoidable dilemma, he had chosen for the latter.

> For me the atmosphere in the church is not mystery but clarity, preaching, the Spirit. I desire not the altar but the pulpit in the choir....The atmosphere in the church may not lose its simplicity and its clarity, what accompanies the preaching of Jonah at Ninevah, of Jesus beside the Sea of Tiberias, of Paul in the hall of Tyre, and of Luther *sub coelo*. It must retain the clarity of the open heavens.[4]

Noordmans had argued in *Herschepping* that the way the incarnation is being discussed is crucial. The incarnation, as we heard him say there, is not about new and beautiful forms but is connected with the brokenness of creation. Jesus is not the "flower of creation," but his coming means that he (and God in him) "has followed us in our fall." This event is from the outset intended "to be taken up in the work of the Holy Spirit"; it does not continue of itself but must be *preached*.

---

[3]   *VW* 4:189.
[4]   *VW* 4:187f.

This insight was determinative for Noordmans's entire presentation of faith as "faith in Jesus Christ." The primary thing for him was that Jesus had gone the way of humiliation and glorification, uniquely, once for all. It is only in that context that thought can focus on the question of how he went that way, i.e., on the human side of Jesus' life. But there, too, what is unique about Jesus may not be lost sight of. It can then be said that Jesus fulfilled the three-fold office of prophet, priest, and king. That may be applied to our lives; our lives may be likened to his. But by definition the three-fold office cannot be continued by us, following on him, in the church, for example, or in culture. Just as the confession of Jesus' kingship may not tempt us to mix Christianity and culture, so may the confession of Jesus priesthood not be the occasion for special liturgical *tours de force*.

> The transitory nature of Jesus' priesthood will be a warning to us in our discussion of Jesus' suffering against sacramentalism and episcopalism, against drowning in mysteries and solemn gestures.[5]

This passage lacks a direct reference to the Liturgical Movement. Still, it is unmistakably in view. We see here the same aversion to elements of mystery which would bring him in 1935 to turn against the incarnational thought of W. J. Aalders. The year *Herschepping* was published, 1934, was also the year the great *Handboek voor de Eredienst* of the Liturgical Union appeared. The arrival of this *Handboek* may have provoked Noordmans to his scattered critical remarks about the "liturgists."

Liturgie

His criticism had remained provisionally limited to those remarks. The passages cited above from *Kerkelijk denken voorwaarde voor kerkorde*, from the Spring of 1938, were friendly, and so far as they were critical, carefully formulated. That was understandable. That brochure was about a (final) defense of the reorganization proposal laid before the General Synod, *vis à vis* a rising storm of criticism. Noordmans was interested in increasing the number of comrades as much as possible against such criticism. Criticizing the Liturgical Movement too sharply, a movement that was part of the "new ecclesiastical front," would only weaken that front. That was not to be done.

---

[5]   *VW* 2:276.

Meanwhile, Noordmans had already let his critical feelings be known, albeit internally, in another context. In January 1938, in the midst of the turmoil of the battle for reorganization, he had taken part in a conference of the Liturgical Union in Hemmen. He had originally not intended to publish his lecture given there ("The Character of Worship"). Later, at the invitation of the publisher, he prepared it for publication. The result was the book, *Liturgie*. It appeared in April 1939, just at the time that the struggle for reorganization approached its (temporary) conclusion. So Noordmans continued that struggle in his own way, contributing as well where he deemed that the battle for church renewal was being taken in the wrong direction by others.

The book's publication occasioned an intense discussion. It was primarily Van der Leeuw who reacted sharply. Van de Pol as well responded through a number of articles. Noordmans did not allow the criticism to go without an answer. The discussion continued from May to September. The Second World War had broken out on September 1, 1939, and it was dimly reflected in the exchanges within the discussion but was not in itself reason to break off the discussion abruptly. Too much was at stake for those involved. What was at stake for Noordmans was nothing less than the right understanding of the Reformed tradition, and behind that the biblical proclamation and the consequences that can be drawn from it. That same year, the contributions of Van der Leeuw, Van de Pol, and Noordmans were collected into a book under the title, *Liturgie in de crisis*. In what follows we will review in summary what Noordmans brought to this discussion. We see the outlines of his theology sketched here as well.

There is a remarkable parallel between Noordmans's (critical) participation in the Liturgical Movement and his involvement in the movement for reorganization. In both cases it was about questions of ordering, giving form. In the case of the liturgy, it was not about ordering the church itself (in its organization) but about ordering the worship of the church. In both cases he argued that the issue of form is about substantive questions, principles. Not only questions of church order, but liturgical questions as well are questions of faith. In both cases as well, he reaches back to the Reformation (in its Reformed character). It is not only in the case of church order (with its structure of offices of the church, the presbyterial system), but in the matter of worship as well that decisions have been made—and that with an appeal to the Bible!—and whoever would diverge from that must know what he is doing! The Reformers had drastically simplified worship, said Noordmans. Not by accident, but on the basis of "a principle...on which one may not go back." Noordmans reproached the Liturgical Movement for transgressing this principle too easily.

Reformed Simplification of Worship

The "simplification" that Noordmans had in mind was the fact that the Reformers had abolished the center of Roman Catholic worship, the Mass (the offering of the Mass as a daily representation—in that sense "repetition"—of the offering of Christ). Calvin did that even more radically than did Luther. Luther had allowed the altar to remain (albeit stripped of its real function as a place of offering). Calvin was consistent and removed the altar from the church.

What remained was a Reformed worship in which Word and sacrament stood at the center, simple, freed from all "attendant ceremonies," as "pillars," "unconnected." The doors of the church are left open to life—for in the Reformed tradition, discipline stands as the "third mark of the true church" next to Word and sacraments. Reformed Christians see the true liturgy, the true service of God, practiced in life. So far as there is something to be offered by us humans, that, too, Noordmans said, happens in life (v. Rom. 12:1). Noordmans cites Calvin, who appealed to the believer not to honor the host of Christ in the church building, but to "be himself the host of God in life."

In this Reformed worship, any attempt at a harmonic, liturgical whole, a "closed system" in which Word and sacraments would fit organically, is abandoned. Such a closed system would mean that worship as a whole would take on a "sacramental" character, as a sort of "cultic system of particular holiness and power," with a "higher degree of divinity than any of its parts, Word and sacrament included, which in turn must be incorporated in the whole." Word and sacrament would then no longer be integral to themselves. An attempt at that sort of liturgical system would give the impression that one could be of the "opinion that the heavenly life had begun."

A similar vision is peculiar to the Greek (Eastern Orthodox) tradition, Noordmans said. There, specifically, the term "liturgy" as denoting worship had already come into use immediately following the New Testament, and it has there the cultic meaning that it also had in Old Testament temple worship. There it was also the case that true service of God found its place in (cultic) worship. That means that one must come from life to the church to serve God. In eastern worship it is as though now, already, "the church stands with the blessed before the throne of God, in his holy presence, falling down to worship." This liturgy "melds heaven and earth."

But this use of the word "liturgy" is not found in the New Testament. It has only later become part of the church of the West. There, one thinks in terms of Latin sobriety. Notions like discipline and office are spoken of; one is cognizant of rules for service that must be executed on earth. Differently from the eastern church, the church of the West saw itself situated in the midst of earthly life, with both feet on the ground. Rome and the Reformation are one on that matter:

> We have reasons to fear the liturgy more than the mass. We are more at home with Rome than with Byzantium. We share with Rome a Latin sobriety, the discipline, the *officium* (office), *ordo* (the sober rule), the *ministerium* (earthly service).[6]

Rome and the Reformation are both part of the western church. That is why here, too, in the churches of the West, faith looks to the offering—offering that is by definition an earthly matter, because it presupposes that God and the human stand in relation to one another and thus are and remain distinct from one another. The only (but important) difference between Rome and the Reformation concerns the interpretation of that offering. Is it brought again by us, in the church, to God? Or was it already brought once for all by Christ, and is that proclaimed by God to us, from heaven to earth? The latter is the position of the Reformation. But this difference does not eliminate the essential agreement between the two.

The Liturgical Movement and the Eastern Church

Shortly before, in his *Kerkelijk denken*, Noordmans had still spoken of the Liturgical Movement as a "catholicizing expansion." But over time he had begun to put the matter differently. The Liturgical Movement does not desire a return to Rome, he said. It was often reproached for that, but Noordmans called that a misunderstanding. It does not attempt the reestablishment of the Mass and the offering of the Mass. Certainly, though, it claims that the simplification brought about by the Reformed tradition has gone too far. One works for an experience of worship as mystery, an experience that is a forceful reminder of the worship of the eastern church.

In doing so, one is inspired by the Anglican Church and the liturgical renewal within it. The Anglican Church has in fact occupied a peculiar, mediating position between Rome and the Reformation

---

6   *VW* 6:54.

from its earliest days: it has on the one hand a confession of faith that can very well be read in a Reformed manner, and on the other hand a Catholic structure of offices (of bishops in apostolic succession). And it has always seen itself connected with the church of the first centuries. Anglican worship does not have the offering of the Mass in a Catholic sense, but it does maintain an "altar" within the church and has an important element of praise and worship. The Liturgical Movement desires to import just that, Noordmans argues, into the Dutch Calvinist church services and thereby correct what is seen to be an abnormality here.

> Whoever supposes that an altar is present in the worship and does not offer together with Rome has to divinize worship, to have it take place as if the congregation stands with the blessed before the throne of God, in his holy presence, falling down to worship.[7]

Worship then becomes a mystery play. In the liturgy one senses oneself taken up into the conversation among the angels and saints.

To those who have adopted "With all saints" as their slogan Noordmans asks critically, "Which saints do you mean?" He fills in the answer himself.

> They are, if I am not mistaken, those Peter, James, and John would also gladly accompany when they talked about making the three tabernacles. They are the saints with haloes or the angels on the front of the organ. The saints through whom the incarnation extends itself or the angels who represent the holy liturgy in the cloister of Athos. Jesus did not find that to be a good thing. These saints in the gospel only peek around the corner. And they do so because they are interested in a different sort of saints, without halo. Those on behalf of whom Jesus offers himself. Magdalene, Matthew, the murderer on the cross. They do not extend the incarnation, but rather hear of it.[8]

The Incarnation Proclaimed

Here we stumble upon the most fundamental point in Noordmans's critique of the Liturgical Movement, that it arises from the notion that the incarnation extends itself in the church and its worship. We already heard him resist this notion in his *Herschepping*,

[7]   *VW* 6:54f.
[8]   *VW* 6:133.

and in his discussion of W. J. Aalders's *De incarnatie*. He does so here again and more clearly so.

Those who talk of a "continuation" of the incarnation, says Noordmans, presuppose that the incarnation was the assumption of a form. A form, a configuration, can indeed extend itself, take on a further configuration. But that the Word has become "flesh" means, Noordmans says, precisely *not* that it has taken on a configuration. Crib and cross are one. Already at the incarnation we have to think immediately of Golgotha, and "on Golgotha all configurations and forms perish." The incarnation meant an offering, and offering does not extend itself; it is brought (once) and therewith the action of bringing the offering ceases. So the incarnation has taken place once, on our behalf. The thought of a "continuation" of the incarnation among us is thwarted through the gospel of Jesus' ascension. Christ is now "with his altar and offering in heaven." And as offering,

> *the incarnation...continues...coming...from above*, in that it is taken up in the outpouring of the Holy Spirit, so that it does not mysteriously rustle through the world but must be proclaimed to everyone in his own language with a clear voice.[9]

This is the reason the Reformers abolished the offering of the Mass and furthermore distanced themselves from Roman Catholic worship. They have thus drawn the correct inference:

> There is no religion without offering. But its absence and with it the absence of the altar is a proof that the direction of the act of offering is turned around....The offer comes in preaching to us, like grace. It does not flame upward from our altar to God.[10]

God's Presence in Worship

Preaching is thus central. The Liturgical Movement may prefer to speak of the sacramental character, or even the mysterious character, of worship, but worship has principally a word-character for Noordmans. Naturally, the sacraments too have their place. But that is not in conflict with the word-character of worship.

> For us Protestants it (is) the external Word in worship that is the place of meeting with God...and in particular the vocal Word,

---

9   *VW* 6:125.
10   *VW* 6:123.

whereby, however, the sacraments remain a kind of word....The sacraments (are) no *Fremdkörper* [foreign body] in the service. Still it is not they, but the Word, that determines the liturgy....The sacraments must stand in the realm of the vocal Word and not the other way around. Luther expressed that when he said that "the power of worship exists in the words of Christ."[11]

Noordmans here sees himself standing diametrically opposed to the Liturgical Movement, which seeks the character of the sacramental, such that "life breaks through in it." Well,

This dynamic realism that finds its origin in Greek liturgy should clear the field for a different kind of realism, as people understand it when things are called by name. The sacrament must thus not be concerned with the categories of life, power, activity. It remains a speaking, a naming. In baptism we receive our names. And in the Lord's Supper Jesus addresses us in the words of institution.... Reality does not break through in the sacrament but it is called by its names.[12]

In agreement with the Liturgical Movement, Noordmans is willing to speak of a "presence of God in worship." But he feels mistrust when a *praesentia realis*, "real ('objective') presence" is spoken of in this connection. He says critically,

One would want to know what that "realis," that *real* in the presence of God, means precisely, and what "matter" in distinction from the "word" intends to express here. When God is present here differently than in the Word, for hearing, for faith, how is that so then?[13]

He resists the thought that we would, by means of our liturgy, have God's presence at our disposal. As if we could say "that God goes to church when we do"! No,

The presence of God is sovereign and thus particular...his presence is not self-evident or objective; it remains a demonstration of grace. Thus it cannot be grasped in a univalent, one particular sense. This presence has its degrees and its variabilities. It is

[11]   *VW* 6:86f.
[12]   *VW* 6:73.
[13]   *VW* 6:76.

different in the Word and different again in the sacrament. It differs at Christmas, Easter, and Pentecost. It is there more at one time than another. It is not the same for all.[14]

One would do better to speak of a "real confrontation" than of a *praesentia realis*. In that way liturgy cannot be elaborated into a complete system but it has

> Necessarily to be seen as fragmentary....in a way that it had been from the outset of the Reformed Church. An organic comprehensive whole with a fixed mystical core in which the presence of God inextricably coheres with particular liturgical actions of the congregation is...unthinkable. We do not have such a *living,* breathing worship that invites biological description.... God can be absent in the service and silent in the sermon. He can also be deaf to the prayers and to the choir's anthem. The presence of God is...an answer to faith. It can never be the result of the practice of a number of rituals....Even when we do not scorn the means, they remain means of grace. And the means which he uses are his means, and not ours....We cannot take God prisoner in the liturgy.[15]

This makes a Reformed practice of religion precarious. So, is a genuine liturgy possible? Is there "a *place* to be found outside the inward human...where God and the human meet each other? Certainly, said Noordmans, the congregation

> is...where the Holy Spirit is, and the Holy Spirit...where one preaches Christ. So the place of meeting comes to lie in the Word. It is not completely turned inward and spiritualized. There remains a place of meeting. But the notion of "place" must be shifted from creation to the gospel and thus obtain an eschatological meaning. In the church we no longer have proper *ground* under our feet. We stand there on the foundation of apostles and prophets and what we must do there is more to *listen* than that we should know. A "liturgical spirit" can do nothing other than to secularize this place. It must be driven out.[16]

---

[14]   *VW* 6:78.
[15]   *VW* 6:79f.
[16]   *VW* 6:85.

Word and Sacrament

We realize again that, for Noordmans, the sacrament is understood under the notion of the Word; indeed, he calls the sacrament "a sort of words." That does not mean that to him Word and sacraments are equal. But in identifying the distinction between the two, he takes a different path than that of the Liturgical Movement. There, the inclination is to judge that the distinction between Word and sacrament lies in different senses: the sacrament is seen (and touched and tasted), the Word is heard. Thus, this distinction is reduced to the distinction between eye and ear. In opposition to this approach, Noordmans maintains,

> One must not give attention in the first place to the form under which they come to us, but to the message that they bring to us...I.e., one may not approach them from creation....They must be distinguished spiritually, according to the will, wisdom, and mercy of God who lays on his children his promises in two ways.... We must speak of the relation between Word and sacrament not from creation, but from Pentecost.[17]

How are the two ways then to be distinguished? Noordmans maintains that the sacrament (in its double configuration as baptism and Lord's Supper) "appears to stand more deeply in need and sin than the Word." It touches us humans where we cannot be completely reached through ordinary preaching. It addresses us in "a state of our sinful existence, which is difficult psychologically for preaching to approach."

Pursuing this last point further, Noordmans argues that the sacraments are involved "at the extremities of life, birth and death." He sees baptism involved in the first, the Lord's Supper in the second. In baptism we are addressed as from our birth imprisoned in sin—and yet saved. In the Lord's Supper we are told that we may share in Christ's death, that we have died with him and may rise to new life.

> In that sense one could say that the sacraments are still *truer* than the Word. They are like the *Amen* after the *Our Father*...whereby the Spirit raises the promises of God beyond the psychological mediation of the Word....So the sacraments are bearers of the mercy of God to the extremes, where "reason fades" and where the Spirit can make itself hardly understandable to the soul. They are torches in the night.[18]

---

[17]   *VW* 6:68f.
[18]   *VW* 6:73-75.

Noordmans distinguishes between Word and sacrament in yet another way. We remember how he emphasized that true liturgy for Reformed Christians, true service of God, finds its place in life, on the street. This agrees with the New Testament, in which the word "liturgy" appears as an indication, not of Christian worship, but of Paul's missionary work (see for example, Rom. 15:16). In this apostolic work of mission, the Word takes its course through the world.

Now Paul is active not only as apostle, but also as pastor; where he had been preaching in mission, he also establishes churches, with offices and ministries.

> Paul (had) not only raced from place to place with the torch of the gospel until Jesus came, but...he (viewed) it at the same time his vocation...to do something in order that those who had become enlightened would also be warmed by the bond of peace. Along with faith victorious over the world also came ecclesiastical love, the principle of true catholicity.[19]

From place to place Paul appoints elders and deacons, or he gives prescriptions for the celebration of the Lord's Supper. It was presumed that the celebration of the Supper would find its place within the congregation. The Word travels all over the world, but the sacraments have specific pastoral significance. Noordmans even calls the Lord's Supper "the center of the formation of the local congregation" and the "center of Sunday worship."

> The Word (can) also turn inward to become pastoral and there meet the sacrament. But it may not do this, as the sacrament does, in order to find the rest there, to which the sacrament has been attuned from its beginning....When it finds rest in the pastoral, it would give itself up to imprisonment. At most it can take a rest there, but it must always keep in mind its peculiar eschatological character. Its extremities connect heaven and earth and embrace the whole of humanity. They also embrace the sacrament, liturgy the church. The Word rests for a while in the pastoral, but it remains a traveler and it does not forget that it began as an instrument for mission.[20]

The sacrament does not have the character of the traveler. It is from the outset instituted for the pastoral communion and finds its goal therein.

[19]   *VW* 6:126.
[20]   *VW* 6:135.

Genuine Reformed Liturgy

The Lord's Supper is the central point of worship, instituted for pastoral communion. In his successive discussion with Van der Leeuw, Noordmans said that with this thesis he had "run more or less against Calvin." So advocating for the independence of the sacrament he drew new inferences from the Reformed doctrine of the sacraments. Inferences that brought him, surprisingly, again close to what had been emphasized from the side of the Liturgical Movement. How does this notion relate to what was at that time (and to a large extent still is) the average practice of the Lord's Supper in Reformed congregations? The situation there appeared (appears) to be the opposite of what Noordmans had envisioned; the Word was present every Sunday and the sacrament only now and then. But, said Noordmans, that cannot be the end of the matter. The sacraments are not as unimportant in congregational life as they appear. Look only to the practice of catechesis:

> The entire catechesis, the education of the children of the congregation, takes place between the sacraments. The young are not raised to be missionaries, but to remain. The catechumens learn...to sit at the Lord's Table.[21]

Was Noordmans an opponent of the Liturgical Movement? He called himself rather an "outsider"—but with great interest for what was happening with the movement. We may not forget that as late as the spring of 1938, in his *Kerkelijk denken*, he considered this movement to be one of the renewing factors that he considered an expression of a "strong enlivenment of the ecclesial consciousness." As he would write (in a short article in 1947, as an aside), he had once been invited to preach in a service of the Duinoordkerk at The Hague, cradle of the Liturgical Movement. He had on that occasion certainly been able to overcome his "liturgical reservations." The only thing that had kept him from accepting the invitation was that as preacher he had to wear a robe there. That "remained an obstacle." Noordmans saw the robe as an academic garment and thus as not belonging in church:

> I certainly know doctors of theology...But our *church* doesn't know them....Before the Word we all stand equal....From an intuitive aversion to the doctorate in the church I have never worn a robe in my more than forty years of ministry....No one has a lease on the truth in the church.[22]

---

[21]   *VW* 6:189.
[22]   *VW* 6:309.

He apparently judged a robe as a liturgical garment, as a garment of the office, to be out of place. But that did not make him an "antiliturgist."

The insight that "we...cannot take God prisoner in the liturgy" still did not keep him from speaking of "the presence of God in worship," as we heard. He expressly resisted notions (of one like Schleiermacher, for example) that would envision the liturgy only as a question of human virtuosity or of religious art. If it all came down to that, nothing really would happen in worship. And that precisely is the point, even for the "most ascetic Puritan," that "in the church" "a particular grace is given." "The Reformed desire *genuine* liturgy." Noordmans speaks here for himself as well.

After *Liturgie in de crisis* (1939), the collection of contributions from Van der Leeuw, Van de Pol, and Noordmans on the occasion of Noordmans's book, the discussion for the most part fell silent. In 1940, Van der Leeuw published his *Liturgiek*, arranged as a systematic manual in matters of liturgical questions. In passing there is also a reference to Noordmans. With few articles written in 1943 and 1944, Noordmans entered a discussion with J. N. Bakhuizen van den Brink, professor of church history in Leiden and a prominent leader in the Liturgical Movement. But only after the war would the discussion be taken up again, this time more broadly.

Then the Netherlands Reformed Church as such would begin to move and develop initiatives that included the liturgical terrain. They would not always agree with Noordmans's insights, but his insights would continue to have influence. They are too fundamental to remain outside the scope of any liturgical reflection.

CHAPTER 12

War Years: Critical Notes at the Onset of Church Renewal

The Outbreak of the War

In February 1939, Noordmans was engaged with a new periodical (a semimonthly paper), *Woord en Wereld*. The founders were primarily those active in the proposal for reorganization that had been rejected by the synod in August 1938. They hoped to continue the struggle for a confessing church by means of this magazine. Inspired by the new theological thinking of Barth, they also wished to pay attention to current questions of state and society. Noordmans was invited to take a place on the editorial board. He gladly accepted the invitation. From its first number and to the end of 1940, he oversaw a regular chronicle of church affairs. At the beginning of 1941, the occupier would ban the paper.

Naturally the approach and outbreak of the war did not go undiscussed in the chronicle of events. In June 1939, Noordmans had written on Germany. There was in that country, he maintained, "a totalization raised to the extreme on every terrain." Thus, it becomes ever more difficult for the church to remain itself. The extreme atmospheric pressure in which Christian life of faith finds itself demands more than human power to resist. No wonder that one sometimes...hears of a certain weariness.[1]

Even in the Netherlands, he writes in October 1939, church life stands in the balance.

> We are forced to give account of the hope that is within us and of the grounds on which it rests. A number of loose props have fallen away....We know that there is a two-fold citizenship. The one finds its center of gravity in heaven, the other on earth. But the *literal* meaning of these biblical truths throws us off balance and has us doubt ourselves....We hope to *remain without* and set our hopes on that. And yet we do not know that the hope which is in us can withstand oppression....Can the church exist on earth concurrent with hell? Is it possible to hold worship in a trench? Or to preach the gospel through gas masks?...Will the church always and everywhere find it possible to adapt? Will it have to train to live its life under every system?...Already many consciences have been vexed by these questions, including the preparation for war....One can withdraw only in a limited way. One can avoid looking for work in places where one, as at some places of (great) industry, can't help but stare the apocalyptic beast in the face. But that is to deceive oneself. For the beast remains our watchdog, our security. Or what comes down to the same thing, the hound of hell, death....There is silent confusion over the fact that prophesy, the church as a great, leading, shaping power, appears to be finished. Politics and material violence wash over us as if they alone have the kingdom and as if there is not a *two-fold* kingdom. The state feels the church as a threat. Will...the...church...be driven back to its sources, to suffering and prayer, find again its own essence and place holiness resolutely above security?[2]

Kraemer: The Church in a New Situation

"Remaining without" did not appear to be possible. The question, "whether the hope that is within us can withstand oppression," became concrete after May 10, 1940. The internal battle among church parties

---

[1]   *VW* 4:257.
[2]   *VW* 4:266-69.

was at one stroke made secondary. The measures promulgated by the German occupier would repeatedly compel the Reformed Church (as well as other churches) to take a public position. The synod would do what it had previously understood itself unauthorized to do: speak in the name of the church, protest. Against the ever more naked oppression of the Jews. Against the way the occupiers attempted to force the ideology of National Socialism on the Dutch population. Against the arbitrary way the occupiers acted. Against the injustice to which Dutch citizens, particularly the Jews, were subjected. These protests in themselves would bear a confessing character. Perhaps they were not always sufficiently clear and courageous. However that may be, the synod would function in a way that one had not previously thought possible and was absolutely not foreseen in the regulations. And movement would happen on the front of the struggle for the reorganization of the church, the struggle which had just only recently, in 1938 and 1939, come to a halt.

An important stimulus on that front was given by H. Kraemer, who as a linguist (and thus a nontheologian!) was a professor of religious history at Leiden and who previously was in missionary service in the East Indies. He was one of the founders of the periodical mentioned above, *Woord en Wereld,* and, like Noordmans, a member of its editorial board. In February 1940, he had written an article in that periodical on the reorganization of the church. In it he had maintained that the struggle for reorganization in the Reformed Church had thus far been too much a matter of professors and ministers. That would have to change. One would have to cease work, at least provisionally, on a new, official, church order. That only provokes greater discord.

According to Kraemer, what was important was that the congregations and their members see the church again as something that concerns themselves. And that they have an eye for the *vocation* of the church, including its relation to society. The church is not so much a matter of formulae as it is of lived faith. Everything must be directed to that. That should also be the synod's business, and it must express itself on such matters. In its contemporary configuration, as a small administrative body, it would of course not be able to do so. But it could call together a broad church gathering of experts to exist alongside itself. This body, consisting of an equal number of lay people and office-bearers, could then offer advice in the name of the church on the question of what the church must say and do. Kraemer referred to his experiences in the East Indies. There, in the 1930s, a similar group had been called together by the church administration of the Protestant

Church. It had led to church renewal there. Could not something like that happen in the Netherlands as well? He made an appeal along those lines: Let the classes, church councils, free groups of office-bearers, and lay people formally request that the synod make such a broad gathering possible!

This appeal did not appear to fall on deaf ears. In its meeting of July 1940, the synod had a series of requests from around the nation on the table, all inspired by Kraemer's suggestion. In the context of the new emergency situation presented by the German occupation, these requests were all the more pressing. The synod granted the request. A broad gathering was convened that would function as a "commission for ecclesiastical consultation." Kraemer's idea that at last half its members be lay people/non-office-bearers was certainly not agreed upon. But lay people and office-bearers both did in fact gather from all sectors of the church.

Naturally, Noordmans was among those named to the commission. But of the nineteen who had been invited, he was the only one who declined nomination. Membership on the commission would bring with it a great deal of travel for him, coming as he was from distant Laren; he apparently deemed that too difficult. In one of his letters he would speak of the "geographic isolation" in which he found himself "most recently" (December 1941). That was also the reason why he stepped down as author of the chronicle for *Woord en Wereld* in January 1941 and did not accept the request that he work as the author of the chronicle for the *Weekblad van de Nederlandse Hervormde Kerk*. "I am not in the position to have sufficient information." Faulty train connections also played a part. In general, the war years would dramatically reduce Noordmans's activities.

His absence from the commission for ecclesiastical consultation meant that he had stepped out of the center of action. Henceforth, he would observe the process of church renewal from the sidelines.

The commission for ecclesiastical consultation met, under Kraemer's chairmanship, for the first time August 27, 1940, and established a number of work groups. Other church members, from the breadth of the church, were also invited to participate in these groups. One of the work groups was *Kerk en Gemeenteopbouw*, again under the leadership of Kraemer himself. It went to work initiating discussions among parties of the church throughout the nation. The term *gemeenteopbouw* (in contradistinction from *Kerkopbouw* of the 1930s) connoted that the group was concerned with the realization of Kraemer's plea: that church renewal should become a matter of the congregations, and congregational members, themselves.

The Path to a New Church Order

Following on this approach, a new start began still later in the preparation of a new church order, the very thing that had been the center of so much struggle in the 1930s. The work was cautious, step by step. First, in 1942, a commission was constituted that was given as its task the drafting of a "work order," a transitional set of regulations. On that basis, prior to any further renewal, a broad "General Synod" could meet that would replace the existing (small, administrative) synod and could truly represent the entire church.

Noordmans was not a member of this commission either. This time his absence was the result of decisions made elsewhere. With the exception of its chair, P. Scholten, a lawyer and professor in Amsterdam, no one was appointed to the commission who had earlier been active in proposals for reorganization or who had been involved in the opposition to proposals for reorganization. This was done to avoid having the new project shackled by old controversies.

The commission presented its proposal in 1944, and the synod accepted it that same year. Only following the liberation could the provincial synodical administrations offer their opinions. Unlike in 1938, they accepted the proposals, even by a large majority. Thus, the church administrative bodies agreed to their own liquidation to make way for a new, truly ecclesiastical structure.

On the basis of these decisions, a new style of synod met October 31, 1945, a broad synod, consisting of representatives from classical gatherings. It immediately gave the go-ahead for work on a new church order. A commission was again established for that purpose, consisting of the same people as the previous commission, complemented with members from the executive committee of the (new) synod. Noordmans, a pioneer in church order from the 1930s, again remained on the outside.

Only in October 1946, when a place came open through the unexpected death of its chair, Scholten, was Noordmans appointed to this commission. By then the commission's activities had gone quite far. The complete proposal for the church order would be offered to the synod in November 1947. Noordmans thus was able to share the commission's work only in part.

After several rounds of discussion, the proposed church order was accepted by the synod in December 1950, again by a large majority; the church order became effective May 1, 1951. Thus, church reorganization became a fact.

The new church order started from the view of the Reformed Church as a Christ-confessing *volkskerk*. The notion of the "apostolate" of the church stood at the center. That concept intended to emphasize the missionary existence of the church, its being sent into the world. The relevant article envisioned this apostolate involved not only with the nations (overseas mission), but also with the society of the Netherlands itself. Concurrently, it envisioned the apostolate including the vocation of the church, "in expectation of the kingdom of God," to turn toward "government and people," "to direct life by God's promises and commands."

The article on the "confessing" of the church followed the article on the "apostolate." It states that the church confesses Jesus Christ as Lord, and does so "in communion with the confession of the fathers" (contained in the classic confessional documents), but it does so today and "ever again," "conscious of its responsibility for the present." Thus, this confessing, too, happens before the world in the context of current questions—so it was supposed. It is itself really a form of apostolate. As was said to the synod (by the secretary of the synod, K. H. E. Gravemeyer): "One notes that confessing is something that matters only as one is sent into the world." By placing the church's confessing in the context of the missionary vocation of the church, party differences could be viewed in a new light and (partially) overcome.

This emphasis on the apostolate validated Kraemer's position. He had argued already in 1940 that a church that would again concentrate on its communal vocation would of itself relativize the internal battle (over confession) and so would result in spiritual renewal.

Critical Notes on *Gemeenteopbouw*

As has been noted, Noordmans stood on the sideline during the entire process of renewal. Still, he followed the course of events as closely as possible. Where he deemed necessary, he expressed his thoughts. He could not unreservedly support *Gemeenteopbouw's* course and the theology of the apostolate that had emerged so strongly. It is possible that that also played a part in his decision in the summer of 1940 not to accept the invitation to membership on the commission for ecclesiastical consultation.

He had for a long time admired Kraemer as a missionary. We saw (chapter 9) that for him (and for *Kerkopbouw* at that time) mission was of great significance, especially in view of the self-understanding of the church. His meeting with Kraemer will have decisively contributed to that insight. In the 1930s, he spoke at church meetings on "the church as a mission problem," as he put it "directed by Oegstgeest" (the mission office), persuaded as he was by a pressing request from Kraemer.

In February 1940, speaking at a meeting of supporters of reorganization, he referred, among other things, to the article published that same month in *Woord en Wereld* by Kraemer. He cited it in agreement. Still, he allowed for some critical remarks. That Kraemer would reap the fruit of his experiences in the Protestant Church in the East Indies for use in the Netherlands Reformed Church evoked questions for Noordmans. The Indies is a mission field, he said. There it is about "spiritual development," and one can reach back directly into the Bible. But there has been an established church in the Netherlands for centuries. A tradition has formed here—doctrinally, in confessional documents and dogmatics, and juridically, in church structures. That may not be shoved aside in the struggle for renewal.

> An account must be taken with us of the many spiritual crystallizations of great value. The deep experiences of eternity from the time of the Reformation, the psychological deepening from the era of Pietism, and the value for feeling from the time of the Réveil have given to our church folk an inner development to which we must pay careful attention. One may not place that on the same level as the spontaneous ebullience of well-meaning modern lay people....However much we should value the latter, we would be mistaken when we think that there is sufficient resistance in it to be able to be a basis for edifying the church.[3]

Noordmans thus found that Kraemer with his new proposal was too much of a bull in the ecclesiastical china shop.

Kraemer further explicated his ideas on church renewal in a number of writings. In 1941, he published a brochure, *De nood der Kerk* [The need of the church]. Noordmans, strongly encouraged by Kraemer himself, responded to the copy that had been sent to him by letter (in December 1941). In it he stated his reservations more explicitly. Behind the action inspired by Kraemer, he noted a vision that posited a union of Christ and the church intended to reach back into an "ur-Christian sphere" as described in the gospels, and which would draw the consequences therefrom for the church of the present. According to Noordmans, this raised the threat that the contemporary church would forget that its situation is different from that of the disciples gathered around Christ in the gospels. The church sees the light of day only in

---

[3]   *VW* 5:510.

the book of Acts and the apostolic epistles. There, a new dispensation had begun which went beyond the gospels.

> The presence of Christ has become something different. It is still a reality, but it exists more spiritually....Care is demanded in the preceding matters. When God leads us from the kingdom to the church, we cannot go back....Thus I read...your...thesis that the leading figures must become less theoretical and more filled with energy with reservation. The Christian confession, the ministries, and the gifts have done more for the preservation of the church than expending energy. They have been raised by the Holy Spirit in particular forms and in that "subsistence" we know Christ. We may not go back behind that to begin anew and to wait and see what will come from that. Not on the mission field and *a fortiori* not in the church. Confession, ministry, and the gifts exist.... We now hear with the ear; we believe with the heart and confess with the mouth. In all three there is something of the rectilinear, which you contest....Taken all together I fear that in a so-called ur-Christian sphere, the contours of which were more or less eliminated, unjustifiably great influence would accrue to just those who would happen to put the sphere above the contours.... By an acting in that sphere they would have less trouble from the hindrances—the question of truth and the problems of the church order. Everything would be distorted in a mystical or practical direction....Thereby then...the church order is set aside and ideas and suggestions are brought to the table *à l'improviste* or in commission outside the existing church governance.[4]

Noordmans deemed such a course of events particularly undesirable. In his opinion, the party question could not be solved and true reorganization of the church could not be reached along that way.

In a later letter to Kraemer (January 1942), Noordmans again gave expression to his objections to the straightforward style of the church policy advocated by Kraemer. Certainly, it is about "great changes in our spiritual and ecclesiastical life," but a "connection of clear truth and mystical certainty will have to lead us" in that. "We will have to know that we can do no other." With that he expressed his mixed feelings about the way that in the meantime was taken (under Kraemer's influence) in which the synod, with its energetic secretary Gravemeyer (having taken office in April 1940), attempted to give leadership powerfully and

---

[4]   *VW* 9:681-83.

centrally through, among other means, pulpit messages. Noordmans wrote, "The church may not be led by proclamations and declarations from above. We are not an Episcopal but a Reformed church." And on the synod (still consisting of and functioning by the old rules):

> Our illegitimate synod may not abuse the conditions, which make criticism nearly impossible, to push things through which would otherwise have no chance. It cannot now abdicate, perhaps, but it may not forget that it earlier had not wished to do so. With this in mind its action must remain limited. I would judge a too personal leadership as most objectionable.[5]

Noordmans again articulated his concern over the action of Kraemer and *Gemeenteopbouw* in a discussion at the time of the ministers' meeting of 1944. Kraemer, who shortly before had returned following an imprisonment and nevertheless undiminished in spiritual power, had given the address, "The Reformed Church at the Cross-Roads." Noordmans asked a pressing question: what really is the specific theology of *Gemeenteopbouw?* Is it perhaps the case here that theology is taken in service of a particular program of action? As with the Liturgical Movement, where he opposed its tendency "to take God prisoner in liturgy," so here he stands against the tendency "to organize the Holy Spirit."

Was that really its intention? Kraemer naturally answered in the negative, but he could not shake Noordmans's critical question. He came back to it later, in 1945, in his book, *De roeping der Kerk* [The vocation of the church]. He continually felt the question "like a pistol against the breast." He acknowledged that "deep, constructive criticism is the only thing that can keep the leadership of such a human movement healthy. *Gemeenteopbouw* must foundationally take to heart the poignant warning against sinful pride, yes, well understood, against the violation of the sovereignty of God, which lies within this question; and that: as rendered service."

Post-War Continuation of the Discussion with Kraemer

Following the war, the phenomenon of synodical pulpit messages presented itself much more emphatically. The synod (since 1945 in a new configuration, with a new mandate) expressed itself on a number of societal and political questions. Noordmans did not keep his displeasure over this under wraps. He asked critically (in an article in February 1946): must the proclamation of such messages continue?

---

5   *VW* 9:687.

I am of the opinion to doubt that. They have their place in an episcopal hierarchy. But in a presbyterial church order the ministry is thereby distorted. Besides the message of Jesus, no message of the synod is appropriate. And the office-bearer thereby becomes a bureaucrat. These pieces are programs from a movement which do not belong in the church and wish to take from God's hands the work that he intends to do through the ministry of the Word in the hearts of his people. They usher a secularization into the church service by which the character of the office changes.[6]

He also continued his direct discussion with Kraemer (and *Gemeenteopbouw*) following the war. He did so, among other places, in June 1946, in an article in the *Weekblad van de Nederlandse Hervormde Kerk*, published under the title, "Militia Christi." This, indeed, against the background of fundamental agreement with what, taken as a whole, had already been achieved ("Happily...1816 is now liquidated," he had written to Miskotte in December 1945). The title, "Militia Christi," plays on Noordmans's central reservation, that there is a kind of militarization of faith being executed in the course of thought taken in the discussion. Noordmans saw this tendency already coming to expression in the concentration of the confession of faith into the one exclamation, "Jesus is Lord!" That can, of course, be said; it is even biblical, but it is not to be forgotten that in addition one can exclaim, "Abba, Father!" and "Come, Creator, Spirit!"

> It is the answer to the three-fold revelation which is given in the Bible. When we now bring one Person exclusively forward, our faith suffers harm. A Jesus-church will, when it engages the individual soul, be too sentimental; when it is active in the world it is too organizational, too engaged in plans, too political, too programmatic.[7]

Where one concentrates so much on Jesus that one forgets the Father and the Spirit, Jesus becomes a field marshal and the faith becomes the obedience of faith, a matter for and of soldiers. But "the church is not a barracks." Only where faith is an answer to the triune revelation of God—Father, Son, and Spirit—is there space for greater relaxation, for the notion that the faith is something "for children and not for soldiers." In the New Testament, the Christian is more often called servant, "slave" of Jesus Christ than soldier, slave who has been ransomed. Certainly he is called to obedience, but still, or just so, free.

[6]   *VW* 5:523f.
[7]   *VW* 5:529.

Therein, according to Noordmans, Christianity is the counter-image of Islam. That is the "true soldier-religion." There a "nearly absolute unity and closedness" rules. With agreement, Noordmans cites Kraemer himself, where he had spoken in other publications of Islam as "a medieval form of National Socialism." It is, then, not accidental that the doctrine of the tri-unity of God is passionately rejected by Islam. All the emphasis there lies on the confession of the unity of God. It is just in Islam that one can see "that the simplicity of God can fuse with the simplicity of the obedience of faith into a hardness and an enclosedness in which humanly speaking there is no longer an opening." It is remarkable, says Noordmans, that it is precisely Kraemer who, in his thought and encouragement, as he places faith as faithful obedience in the center and sees the exclamation, "Jesus is Lord," as the quintessence of Christian faith, appears to negate the frightening example of Islam to which he himself had called attention.

Making faith one sided can certainly have its place, Noordmans granted, in "what one with Rome calls an order." Then one directs oneself to one special goal. It demands a special organization. The Reformed churches have always known little organization. Their form of organization was always as sober as possible; "The people...were not mobilized." And that needs correction today.

> Life is...technical, and thus it has often become inhuman, demonic. Our word-churches, in society, in the families, threaten to go under. Over and against that the church may not remain inactive. It is in need of organization in this mechanical age. Perhaps it needs to display some similarity with the orders of the Roman Church.[8]

Thus, something of a movement is needed, an action group. Noordmans reaches back here to his own thoughts, developed in the 1930s. We heard (chapter 9) how at that time he pled for the "mobilization" of the church as a "salvation army." There he used military terms himself. Still, he ends critically:

> The church may...not itself become an order. It has to maintain a broad openness which makes it a womb, in which all equally, actively and passively, have a free view of the last thing promised in the Credo: eternal life.[9]

---

[8]   *VW* 5:534.
[9]   *VW* 5:534.

CHAPTER 13

The Gospel in the Midst of the Horrors of War

Conditions in Noordmans's Personal Life: Mandatory Retirement

Meanwhile, Noordmans had celebrated his seventieth birthday on July 18, 1941. In that same year the synod had accepted a proposal that would make retirement mandatory for ministers. It would begin when one reached the age of sixty-five. However, for ministers older than sixty-five, but who had served less than forty years, a transitional rule was introduced. For them, retirement would begin after forty years of ministry or when they had attained seventy years of age, whichever came first. The new rule went into effect in 1943. In that year, Noordmans reached the milepost of his fortieth year in ministry. At the end of 1943 he was required to retire.

He retired, but not without protest. He had great difficulty giving up his ministry, and there were also practical problems. He would have to move, but where? And under the conditions of war? In a letter to the synod (dated July 24, 1943), he called attention to the "painful" nature of the new rule, which he characterized as a "break with a centuries-old tradition." "In this way, retirement is like an exercise in discipline."

149

At a request submitted by him and several others, the synod enacted an emergency measure. It would be possible for the church council to designate a retired minister as an assistant minister in his old congregation for another six months (with the approval of the church wardens and the classis). This possibility was made use of in Noordmans's case, so he could remain in Laren, remain in residence in the parsonage, and continue his ministerial duties as an assistant minister. He found the fact that he was no longer a member of the church council a difficult pill to swallow. In a letter, he called the half year in which he no longer really held office in the church the most difficult year of his entire life. The situation ate away at his health.

At the end of June, this additional period was at an end. His farewell service was held June 25, 1944. In his farewell sermon, he said that he had shrunk from this as from a mountain, but that he had learned to accept the fact that he must depart. In part, his attitude was a consequence of a hard blow that had struck him and his wife just a month previously (May 25), with the sudden death of their oldest son. Noordmans wrote to Scholten,

> This suffering has overshadowed the earlier one. I can now be somewhat reconciled to my departure from office....I do not feel broken, but touched by the divine will, so that I see human behavior as taken up in a larger context. The sympathy of many church members was so moving, their sadness so like our own, that all bitterness is removed and the divine mercy embraced us therewith in our suffering, including my son, yes, him above all.[1]

A new minister had already been called to Laren, but because of the conditions of the war his arrival was continually delayed (his arrival, in fact, never took place; the newly called minister died shortly before the liberation). So Noordmans continued in his pastoral work, and he continued to live in the parsonage with his family. This would not last long. In November 1944, the parsonage was requisitioned by the Germans for a munitions depot. The Noordmans family had to seek temporary shelter not once, but several times.

The Final Months of the War: Liberation

With the requisitioning of the parsonage, the violence of the war arrived. In letters written shortly after the liberation, Noordmans looked back on recent events and reported what had taken place. "I

---

[1]   VW 9:731.

personally was in danger for my life; at the beginning of March, by an explosion in my immediate neighborhood which caused two deaths." On March 30, 1945, Good Friday, Noordmans led a church service, which included a celebration of the Lord's Supper; the service had to be suspended because of war activity in the immediate neighborhood. The following day, the Saturday before Easter, Noordmans and his wife again found themselves in grave danger; a "volley from a fighter plane went directly through our bedroom." Two days later, in the night between the Monday and Tuesday following Easter, the supply of munitions exploded in the parsonage. "The parsonage is a ruin, and the church is without roof or tower." That same Easter week, the violence would demand still a higher toll: "The village is a ruin because of three days' bombardment. Thirty farm houses have gone up in flames....We (hid) for the three days of the bombardment in a cellar. Happily only two of our citizens died on this last occasion."

On Thursday, April 5, liberation arrived in Laren. A few years later, Noordmans would remember the experience in an Easter meditation (on Ezek. 37, the vision of the dry bones that become alive in the world of the prophet—a symbol of Israel's resurrection):

> I still smell the air of the evening of the liberation...when we crept out of the cellar, the grave in which we had lain for three days. How sweet the world smelled then. The evening had become morning, the first day (Gen. 1:5). It was a sacrament for us, a sign and seal of the Easter gospel.[2]

On Sunday April 8, the Sunday after Easter, Noordmans preached on Luke 24:34: "The Lord is truly risen!" In his sermon, he put into words his feelings at liberation.

> When we crept out of the cellar, the one earlier the other later, we could hardly believe it: *it is over*, the page has been turned. It looked like the gospel. We thanked God that he had given us this salvation. In the darkest months of 1940/41, we had hardly dared believe that a new dawn would appear in our national life. So we rejoiced greatly. And we thank God, deeply moved, for the release of prisoners, the return of those absent. But we do so with trembling. First because of the need in the western part of the nation. A need so much greater than our own....And second, because whoever ventured from his hiding place after the

---

[2]   *VW* 8:137.

liberation and looked out over the village was confronted with a scene of devastation....Some things we learned by experience: under fire, shelling, plundering. We now know, at least in the center of the village, what it means when armed death hammered not with a scythe but a sledge hammer on the house, where we have hidden in the lowest part of the earth, descended into hell. And the fires; many here saw their homes and goods go up in flames and lost the necessities of life.[3]

For Noordmans, too, the joy of liberation was mixed with suffering and care. He wrote about it in his letters.

Our furniture lay strewn about and is for the most part ruined. We must...move again, for the third time. We have barely a *pied à terre*....Under existing circumstances it is scarcely possible to satisfy life's basic needs. Only the scarcity of food was not pressing here. My library lay somewhere in attics and was threatened by the bombardment. Will I ever again have a study and be able to consult books?... My wife and I soldier on, as best we can. We see the future in a subdued light.[4]

"Sinner and Beggar"

In September 1945, "law and order" returned for Noordmans and his family "again from out of the debacle" (as a friend put it in a letter); they established a new home, this time for good, in Lunteren. From there he could again resume work, his writing and reflection.

The experiences of the war, however, continued to influence his work. More than ever he realized that the gospel also is concerned with bodily needs. Here, he saw, is the corrective necessary to the spiritualizing manner by which the church for centuries has preached salvation. Already in his sermon of April 8, 1945, he put it into words.

The question of salvation is often handled as something concerning the soul. Sin and grace. That is the Pharisee and the tax collector (Luke 18:9-14). There is also another parable: the rich man and the poor Lazarus (Luke 16:19-31). Grace penetrates our entire existence. Of course we desire grace, but as a matter of the soul. Spiritual beggars. Not for the entirety of existence. Not Lazaruses. Like the rich man, we would have the page turned. God

---

3   *VW* 7:330.
4   *VW* 9:740f.

has now changed that a bit, shifted life a bit in the direction of the beggar. Now the page can be turned.[5]

He would think through this theme of "sinner and beggar" primarily in an extended meditation under that title (November 1945), a meditation worth particular consideration here. In it he again placed both parables, from Luke 18 and 16, beside each other. They were both well-known parables, he would claim. But

> the first, that of the sinner, had become much more current among Christians than that of the beggar. Every Sunday the church was filled with sinners, but one noted few beggars; they find or, better, found themselves along the roads. When we read the first parable, we knew immediately that it was about ourselves; with the latter we preferred to think of another. It certainly appears that God has desired to change that. He has given the parable from Luke 16 an application that brought many of us to mystical experiences. Bodily need appears to be more closely connected with salvation than we thought. And that the prayer for daily bread in the Our Father precedes the petition for forgiveness of debts, as the parable of the beggar precedes that of the sinner, is less strange to us than it was earlier.[6]

The Rich Man and Lazarus

Of course, the church has always known that the parable of the rich man and the poor Lazarus is in the Bible, but the church has always interpreted it in a spiritualized manner. In the parable of the Pharisee and the tax collector, the two characters are contrasted in such a way that in the tax collector's position—he stood at a distance and prayed for grace—a judgment is made on the position of the Pharisee—who stood erect, convinced of his righteousness, and who as such returned to his home unjustified. But a similar contrast is usually not read in the parable from Luke 16. The usual inclination is to view the rich man and the beggar here just as they are. You can be rich and godless, but also godly; you can be jealous in poverty, but also content. "So the rich man is a lesson for the rich and Lazarus...for the poor." The relation between rich and poor, then, remains out of view.

> The garish colors by which Lazarus's misery is sketched offers no reproach to the resident of the house where Lazarus lies at

---

[5]   *VW* 7:331.
[6]   *VW* 8:15.

the gate. They delineate the individual beggar. That is or was a class in society and thus needs attract little attention from the rich man. Perhaps he lived somewhat joyfully, or nicely, but that did not concern Lazarus. That was something to be criticized by his neighbors.—God can naturally judge, but that still happens on such external things as somewhat too large a income much less easily than over too proud a heart, as with the Pharisee. Salvation is hardly in danger by that. So the figures in this parable remain separated from each other. They do nothing to each other. Between them a chasm had already been established so that the one can not cross over to the other. The chasm was created by providence.[7]

Noordmans claims that this appeal to God's "providence," often made by the church, was a typical specimen of natural theology. It is about how things "happen to be." There is, then, in the relation between humans no longer any movement, no dialectic. In this way, the church has always attempted to blunt the sharp edge ("the sharp arrows") of the gospel.

The "Gospel of the Poor"

But in the long run, that sharp edge is still being felt. The "powerful parable of Luke 16" does not let us rest. A question presses:

Has the church...preached the full gospel? Has it expended too little thought on the Lazaruses and too much on the tax collectors? Must the beggar be saved in precisely the same way as the tax collector? Does the church not turn away many from the gate of heaven by its methodism?...There are great groups of people among whom the contrast between poor and rich has occupied the whole of human existence more than the contrast between humility and pride....I cannot imagine that Jesus thought of the beggar in Luke 16 as a Pauline Christian....Lazarus believes with his sores, with his total misery. His existence is God's creation from a very small angle, but its supplement is heaven. Of course, he too is a sinner; but Jesus does not speak of that with him. His poverty and misery bring him to heaven....Bodily needs stand in the gospels in immediate connection with the coming of the kingdom.[8]

[7]   *VW* 8:17.
[8]   *VW* 8:20f.

God teaches that conclusion to us today, Noordmans goes on. Certainly, the gospel of sin and grace, as the church has learned it from Paul, must be proclaimed. The Reformation has rightly placed that again at the center, and most recently (think of Barth!) it has been given sharper expression than ever. That is a gain. But,

> Besides the tax collector, God asks consideration for Lazarus. Besides the sinner, for the beggar. The dialectic from the parable in Luke 16, long neglected, broke over us and forced us to new reflection....The beggar died and was borne by angels to Abraham's bosom. There are among us those who have read this line from the gospels as for the first time and have drawn comfort from it in a different way than they had been accustomed to seek or to find the comfort of the Holy Spirit.[9]

Is that then too easy? It can be, but need not be. In any case,

> when it pleases God to gather his children in a different way than we think that he must; when it pleases him to place Lazarus, too, in the midst of the church, and not only the tax collector, then we may not resist. In both cases, it remains our Heidelberg Catechism: misery, salvation, and gratitude. But there are two sorts of misery. There is the weariness of the soul and there is the weariness of the body. They are not always connected. *And sometimes they exclude each other.* There are human needs that so occupy the human that inner practices are impossible.... Paradoxically one can say: the beggar does not consider himself a sinner; his poverty takes the place of guilt. There are great groups of people to whom the parable of the sinner has less to say than that of the beggar....There are circles so in touch with life's needs, with struggle for life's necessities, with the hardness of the rich, that their awareness of sin is to a certain extent retarded. God stands a judge beside them, not over and against them.—Or, they disappear into the mass of humanity through their sort of work, that they cannot find the solitariness, the asceticism of the spirit that the life of penance demands....With the oppressed a need will often originate for more immediate comfort than what we call justification....A desire to have the hands, the oil and anointing of the good Samaritan laid on the sores of life....Many will easily understand Jesus' gospel from that side, while they will have

---

[9] *VW* 8:21f.

difficulty with the concentration of faith in the heart alone. They will believe and confess with their entire existence....There is in the Bible a "gospel of the poor," that runs parallel to that of sinners and that also wants to be preached.[10]

Those who have seen this "will note that the parable of the rich man and Lazarus is not a strange element in scripture." Everywhere, including the Old Testament, "we find the gospel of the poor." We "must let these things stand in the Bible and in the gospel."

The Gospel and the Totality of Human Existence

That the gospel, the judging Word of God, and thus faith as well has to do with the totality of human existence was not a new thought for Noordmans. We saw that he made that clear already in 1934, in *Herschepping*'s chapter on belief in the Holy Spirit. But his personal experiences in the final months of the war, the horrors that he and his family had had to endure, urged him to accent this thought all the more powerfully. His meditation, "Sinner and Beggar," also came out of those experiences. The interpretation of the Bible, the focus on proclamation, can never be timeless. It always engages the events of the time and is likewise influenced by them. In a particular context, aspects of the gospel come to light that previously could not be understood in quite that way. Noordmans has enabled us to see what that means in a very gripping way.

---

[10]   *VW* 8:22.

CHAPTER 14

Mature Theology (1): God the Father, the God of the Future

Renewed Contact with Readers

It is astonishing that Noordmans resumed his work of theological publication immediately following liberation from the horrors of the war with characteristic intensity (he was nearly seventy-four years old) from his new residence in Lunteren.

He began negotiations with the publisher Holland in Amsterdam on the publication of a collection of his writings. Earlier plans for publication had not been realized due to war conditions. Now, in a letter (October, 26, 1945), he urged haste: "I would not be pleased to see too long a delay in publication of the work. Could we not begin immediately? For the first time in a year I have my writing table at my disposal....My library is again in place." A week later: "I hope now that I will soon receive the proofs. I long to renew contact with my readers."

That contact would indeed be quickly restored. In 1946, *Zondaar en bedelaar* ["Sinner and Beggar"] appeared, a collection of a number of meditations, many of which had been published in various periodicals between 1912 and 1936. It contained new text at the beginning, published for the first time: the extensive reflection on the two parables from Luke 18 and 16 that was discussed in the previous chapter. It is from this reflection that the title of the book was taken.

Also in 1946 Noordmans was engaged as a coworker in the weekly publication, *In de Waagschaal* [On the scale]. This paper had been established in 1945 at the initiative of Miskotte. It devoted (and devotes) thought to theological, cultural, and political questions inspired by the work of Karl Barth. *In de Waagschaal* would become the vehicle *par excellence* for Noordmans's further publications. In particular, he would write many meditations, beginning at the end of 1947 at Miskotte's urgent request (Miskotte wrote to him: "You can do it! It is yours to do! And you are well-disposed toward us and 'our kind.' There are many ministers among us who also need it.") A meditation became a regular feature under Noordmans's editorship until 1954, and it became the preferred form in which he expressed himself. It became for him a sort of pastorate for his readers, whom he viewed as his congregation. In 1949 thirty-one of these pieces (ten of them on psalm texts) were collected under the title, *Gods Poorten* [God's gates].

In the same year, 1949, two books also appeared from Noordmans's pen. The first was the collection, *Zoeklichten* [Searchlights] (of which we just noted his correspondence with the publisher). This book opens with "Geloven op gezag," from 1921, one of the texts in which the turn in Noordmans's thought in the direction of a more critical theology had begun to appear (see chapter 5 above). Apart from that, texts were brought together in this volume (on faith, life, ecumenism, church order, church and state) from the years 1932-48. The republication of these essays enabled them to exercise their influence anew.

Also to appear was *Het Koninkrijk der hemelen* [The kingdom of heaven]. It was a commentary on that part of the Heidelberg Catechism that deals with the (twelve) articles of the Apostles' Creed. It is thus in itself—following *Herschepping* (1934)—a complete dogmatics. It appeared as a volume in a series of books in which different authors commented on different parts of the catechism.

In 1955 a collection of meditations from *In de Waagschaal* appeared under the title *Gestalt en Geest* [Form and Spirit]. It was broader and richer than the two previous collections of meditations together. This final publication from Noordmans is also the high point of his theological work. A new edition would appear already in 1956, shortly after Noordmans's death.

Study Circle on Karl Barth

Noordmans's post-war activities were not limited to publication. In November 1947 he began a study circle in Arnhem on the theology of Karl Barth. Participants were ministers from Arnhem and its environs. Barth's doctrine of creation was discussed; the first part had appeared in 1945 (which included an extensive review of the biblical creation stories from Genesis 1 and 2). In 1948, the second part came out; in particular it dealt with the human. That, too, was taken up in the discussions.

Earlier we saw (chapter 6) how Noordmans was already intensely busy with Barth's theology in the 1920s and had been in discussion with it, specifically with Barth's *Römerbrief*, his sensational interpretation of Paul's letter to the Romans. Noordmans was a kindred spirit with Barth, but he had never been an uncritical follower. He had maintained his questions and critical reservations. In the meantime, Barth's theology had undergone further development. Barth had begun to write his great work, *Kirchliche Dogmatik*. In it he had moved in a direction, specifically with his doctrine of creation, in which Noordmans could not follow. We will again see how he saw himself pressed to express his criticism of yet another way.

Noordmans could lay all of that on the table in his Arnhem study circle, a group that continued into the 1950s. Not only Barth, but other modern theologians were discussed. It was a rich experience for those who participated.

Involved with the Synod Work Group, "Kerk En Overheid"

Again through these years, Noordmans was to some degree involved in the national policy of the church. We have seen that in 1946 he had been appointed as a member of the Commission on Church Order. This time, the outlines of the proposed church order had already been drawn, but it was an occasion for him to offer his vision yet again. He tendered his assistance in discussions on various proposed provisions: on ecclesiastical offices and assemblies, on questions on the relationship between administration and financial oversight of the church, on oversight and discipline, on the matter of the "apostolate" of the church, on the education of ministers, and on worship. Those who examine the full course of Noordmans's life and work will not be surprised that these matters were dear to him.

From 1946 (until 1950) he was also a member of the synodical working group, "Kerk en Overheid" [Church and government]. Already in 1945 his involvement included the preparation of a pastoral letter to be published by the synod on the death penalty (a theme that was very current because shortly after liberation the death penalty had been temporarily reestablished in the Netherlands in the context of justice for war criminals). He wrote an extensive memorandum on behalf of the work group, in which he disclosed his rejection of the death penalty.

> Even though the death penalty would be biblical...can the church still...advise the state to kill the fugitive from this place of safety?... The government cannot use the principle of *ius talionis* [i.e., the right of vengeance, K.B.], of like for like. Homicide is a public offense. The offender and the state do not stand on equal terms.[1]

The synodical letter on this subject (which went out at the end of 1945) sounded different. It included on the one hand the warning against hate and vengeance, on the other hand the expression that the government, as a servant of God called to maintain justice, "has the right according to God's Word to apply the death penalty in the case of very heavy guilt." Noordmans expressed his disagreement with this synodical witness. He was not enamored with ecclesiastical statements and pulpit pronouncements; in his opinion, such messages must only be made in emergency situations. The church of the Reformation is (differently from Rome!) not a "political body" and thus must not act as such.

Other matters on which Noordmans, in his involvement in the work group, expressed himself were the question of the possibility of the refusal of military service and the significance of the oath (in distinction from the promise). Noordmans wrote in a memorandum on the first theme, "Resistance against 'Command is command' is a spark that must be fanned into flame." In his memorandum concerning the oath, he argued that one must not too easily abandon the oath as the "main pillar of the order of law," but also that one who denies God cannot and must not be asked to pledge an oath.

Proposed Questions for Confession

As a member of the Commission on Church Order, Noordmans was part of the subcommission on liturgical formulae. In the context of preparing a service book (a liturgy) of the church, he offered a proposal for confessional questions in December 1946. These were questions that could function in church services in the public profession of faith.

---

[1]   *VW* 6:557.

The Commission on Church Order discussed them but did not accept them. They were cited later in *Liturgische Handreiking* [Liturgical helps], a publication (1967) from the later Reformed Council for Worship. In this publication the council formulated its own questions, which, however, were close to those suggested by Noordmans. In these questions, proposed by Noordmans, we find his theological vision expressed in condensed form:

> Do you confess yourself a member of the church of Christ, and do you believe that we have a Father in heaven and that his kingdom is at hand?
>
> Do you thus acknowledge Jesus Christ, his only begotten Son, as your Lord and believe yourself to be elect and called to confess him before humans, to strive against sin and the devil, and to offer your life to him?
>
> Do you trust that the Holy Spirit will give you gifts to that end, will comfort you under the cross, and will make you share in the communion of saints?
>
> Do you thus long to sit at the Table of the New Covenant, to lift your heart on high to the Lord with the church, to proclaim his death, to celebrate his resurrection, and to call on his Spirit?
>
> And are you willing to subject yourself to the discipline of the Spirit in the church?[2]

In the first three questions, faith in God the Father, in Jesus Christ the Son, and in the Holy Spirit appear in succession. The pastoral tone is to be noted, which emerges from the way each successive question begins: "Do you confess," "Do you acknowledge," "Do you trust," Do you long."

It is also remarkable that in the first question, on belief in the Father, the creation is not mentioned. Here Noordmans's peculiar vision on "creation," which he had unpacked in *Herschepping*—"creating is separating"—is recognizable.

The indication of the call "to offer your life to him (Jesus Christ)," in the second question, is further to be noted. The accent is on *life* as liturgy that we came across in his book, *Liturgie*, and in his discussion with the Liturgical Movement. The discussion with Kraemer also shows through here. Noordmans wrote in his exposition, "The *militia Christi* which breaks through here cannot result in hypertrophy between the childhood in question I and the brotherhood in question III."

---

2   *VW* 9:776.

At center, in the third question, stands the Spirit, the Comforter, with his gifts. The gifts are what make the confession possible.

As presupposed in the fourth question, the offering (death) of Christ is neither continued nor made present in the celebration of the Lord's Supper but (as it happened once) is proclaimed. This offering is thus not (again) brought from us upward, but rather comes from on high to us. Therein we also recognize his contribution to the liturgical discussions. Noordmans wrote in explanation, "The offering is in heaven and not on the altar. The death of the Lord is proclaimed, i.e., the gospel comes to us in the Word." The appeal to the Spirit, to which the fourth question refers at its close, brings to expression that the presence of God in the church service is not automatic—and at the same time that this constitutes the (graceful) essence of the church service. This is again a core element of Noordmans's vision of the liturgy.

Believing in the Creator Is Believing in the Kingdom of God

The most important and most influential work of Noordmans in the post-war years was what appeared as new work in book form: *Het koninkrijk van hemelen* and his collections of meditations—*Zondaar en bedelaar, Gods poorten,* and (above all) *Gestalte en Geest.* Here the theological lines of Noordmans's earlier work are drawn out further and accents come into focus. Here Noordmans's own theology stands before us as mature work. Two themes in particular are characteristic of these books: First, he rejects speaking of God's creation as "making," "forming." Connected with that is his vision of the coming and work of the Spirit as the real, decisive action of God with us and in the world. We will discuss the latter theme in the following chapter. Here we turn our thoughts to the first theme.

Already in *Herschepping* we came upon Noordmans's adagium, "creating is separating." In other words, that God is Creator means that he judges, namely throws apart, light and darkness, day and night, sea and dry land, the line of promise and the line of curse. We must, Noordmans said there, clear our heads of all thought of "creation" in the sense of beautiful forms, harmony, an unbroken whole, a rose garden in which we can walk about with God. At its deepest, creation is (as the New Testament speaks about it) that God accompanies us to Golgotha and there himself stands under judgment. If we wish to speak at all of "creating," we must realize that we know creation as nothing other than as fallen, as oriented to the cross, as "a light around the cross."

We just heard how, in the first question he had proposed for confession of faith, he does not speak of God as "Creator." In its stead the question speaks about the belief "that his kingdom is at hand." In *Herschepping* he had already said that "believing in God the Creator is believing in the kingdom of God." This thought is sharpened in Noordmans's commentary on the catechism. Not for nothing is its title *Het Koninkrijk der hemelen.*

The Heidelberg Catechism, following the Apostles' Creed, does talk about God as "Creator" (Sunday 9). In that connection, a separate paragraph is dedicated (Sunday 10) to God's "providence." The catechism identifies providence as included in God's being as Creator; that God "has created heaven and earth out of nothing" also includes the fact the he "sustains and rules by his eternal counsel and providence." And this divine "sustain and rule" is supposed to mean that "leaf and blade, rain and drought, fruitful and unfruitful years, eating and drinking, health and sickness, wealth and poverty, yes all things come to us not by accident by from his fatherly hand." That beckons us "to be patient in adversity, thankful in prosperity, and to have good confidence in the future" in God the Father who loves us.

This passage forces Noordmans to lay his cards on the table in his vision of faith in God "the Creator." He notes that in the catechism—as well as in the Apostles' Creed—God is rightly confessed immediately as "Father." And this Father

> is the Father from the *kingdom of heaven.* He is much more the God of the future than of the past. In the creation he allows his sun to rise over the evil and the good, and rain on the just and the unjust (Matt. 5:45). He does that, as it were, with his left hand....But his good favor is to give to his own the kingdom (Luke 12:32). The other things will be given to them as well, more or less carelessly.[3]

Had the authors of the catechism considered this, they would also have understood that thoughts of the "creation" and "general providence" are not appropriate here, that these are more an expression of "pagan religion." In this connection Noordmans alludes to the time of the German occupation, the era of National Socialism in which one readily spoke of "providence." It should be remembered, he said,

> how in the most pagan period of our history since Willibrord established the church here, reservations were introduced if someone took providence less seriously, but not if he shoved God's law to the side, to be completely silent about the kingdom of God.[4]

3   *VW* 2:457.
4   *VW* 2:458.

It strikes Noordmans that the catechism rarely speaks of the kingdom of God. That has to do, he says, with the one-sided nature of the Reformation. It concentrated, in the articulation of salvation, on the inner need, on the "soul's need," of the human. This one-sidedness could have been broken through if, along with the belief in God the Father, one had emphasized the "gospel of the kingdom." Then,

> the external misery from the gospels [would] have been more prominently in view. The need of the blind, the crippled, the paralyzed, the deaf, the poor, the demon-possessed. And that not from the viewpoint of general providence, which the pagans also confess, but in connection with the "at hand" of the kingdom of heaven. By the connection with this kingdom the righteousness of God would also have come to the fore with regard to this kind of misery, the Lazarus-misery (Luke 16).[5]

...and thus not only with regard to the "misery of sin and guilt, the tax collector-misery" (Luke 18).

We see here that the theme Noordmans struck in his meditation, "Zondaar en Bedelaar," was not secondary but was a core element in his theology.

Not Faith in Providence, But Expectation of the Kingdom

The separate paragraph in the catechism (Sunday 10) on "providence" brings Noordmans to dedicate a separate chapter to this question in his commentary. It strikes him that the catechism highlights "providence" as a motif about confidence in God and thus freedom from all cares. So it focuses thought on precisely those matters (such as eating, drinking, clothing) that Jesus denotes in Matthew 6:25-34 as "things that the Gentiles seek," while he, in contrast, appeals to his followers to seek "first the kingdom of God and his righteousness." Jesus' intention, says Noordmans, is "not to quiet cares, but to wake cares," namely cares "which belong to a citizen of the kingdom of God."

One could certainly speak of God's "providence," but as "concentrated on the red thread that runs through the entire Bible" and thus "focused on the great goals of God in salvation history." It is clear that it is about "a precarious work of God" here, "that is not completed with turning an unfruitful year aside." The work of God is attacked by counter-powers—the devil and his legions. Those mindful of that see "not only creation, but providence as well result in separation" and

[5]   *VW* 2:459f.

thus in a judgment in which the just are separated from the unjust, as Matthew 25:31-46 shows. This is a different providence from that which one thinks one can derive from the biblical text (Matt. 5:45) on God "who allows the sun to rise on the evil and the good."

In the Sundays dedicated to "creation" and "providence," the catechism speaks not only unbiblically, but also in terms and thoughts of a time long past.

> There have perhaps been centuries, such as the eighteenth, in which this half-natural theology gave satisfaction to souls seeking harmony. When, however, two-thirds of Lisbon was destroyed by an earthquake on November 1, 1755, these souls nearly lost their piety.—In our century the state of spirits is different and what scandalizes is also of a different kind. It has less, or even no, relation to natural theology and a doctrine of providence which is oriented towards that. It is not derived from creation as such, and the difficulty that the modern humans had with the conflict between the Bible and natural science is outdated. One comes across it only in circles that are outlived. The real scandals of our century concern the kingdom of God, because it does not come.[6]

Still, we hope for the coming of that kingdom. Only in that hope can we bear the anxiety in which we live today. That hope "rests on the promise of the gospel." And it is not a hope "for the long term." As we know, Jesus himself said that the kingdom of heaven is at hand! Thus it is not proper for the church to place the kingdom "in the final article of her confession, or at the back of the catechism," "but at the outset or in the middle." We have nothing to offer for a providence faith (pious, but oh so weak).

> Nowadays, it is not about rain and drought, prosperity or adversity, wealth or poverty. It is about public righteousness, about truth or lies, about religion or idolatry...about love or hate, murder or turning the other check, about war or peace.[7]

In the unbiblical, in fact pagan, language of the catechism on "providence" Noordmans saw one of the consequences of the doubtful way of speaking about "creation." The Heidelberg Catchism is in general an outstanding book of teaching that has proven to be of excellent service to the church for a long time. Noordmans would certainly not

6   *VW* 2:469.
7   *VW* 2:469f.

deny that; however, in these passages on "creation" and "providence" he sees the catechism as having gone out of tune.

Barth's Doctrine of Creation Critically Discussed

But is Noordmans not too rigorous here? Does he not radically cut out what is in fact an element of biblical proclamation? Must not "creating" still mean "forming," as it can be derived, for example, from the texts of the creation stories? Does Genesis 1 not say that an earth originated under heaven, populated by animals and humans? Does the traditional creation faith not have it at least partly correct?

Karl Barth saw it much as Noordmans did: the Word of God stands critically over against reality. He too desired a radical avoidance of the mixture of Christian faith with pagan religiosity. Still, that did not keep him from developing a "doctrine of creation" in his dogmatics. Noordmans followed that with intense thought. As we saw, he dedicated the discussions in his Arnhem study circle to just that. He could not, he explained there, support Barth in this way of thinking. Indeed, he found it an occasion for renewed and sharper criticism of Barth.

To understand his position well, we must look briefly at Barth's doctrine of creation. In this part of his dogmatics as well, Barth wanted to take seriously the fact that God cannot be known other than in Jesus Christ. But Barth is convinced that just the witness of Jesus Christ *implies* the proclamation that God the Father has created heaven and earth. Because it is through Christ that we know that God is Immanuel, "God-with-us"—thus not a God-alone, but a God together with. So *from that* we clearly see that there is something other besides God, a world, a reality, a humanity, the world in which the Word became flesh. It is in Christ that we not only learn to know God but the human as well, in the midst of the world. Thus, whoever believes in Jesus Christ *must* also confess God as Creator. That, then, is not philosophy, let alone paganism, but an acknowledgment that the reality in which we live and in which we share is available for God *as a workplace and material for his work*. Said more precisely, creation is the space in which the history of the covenant of God with the human in Jesus Christ (can and) does unfold. As Barth himself formulated it, creation is "the outer ground of the covenant," fully set out in relation to that covenant. That is the tenor of the first creation story (Gen. 1-2:3). Put the other way around, the covenant is "the inner ground of creation," the essential reason why it, the creation, exists. That is the tenor of the second creation story (Gen. 2:4ff.). And from the thesis that Jesus Christ does not only show us who God is, but also who/what the human is, Barth subsequently develops an entire view of the human. Looking to Jesus you see what human being is: human-before-God, human-before-fellow human. Barth thus maintains that what the human being is as such, what he is meant to become, can be read off Jesus' human being.

Noordmans deemed these considerations completely wrong. In the text that he wrote in 1947 for his study circle, he identified (in telegram-style) his main criticism:

> that Barth, when he goes from Jesus Christ to creation, bends outward too far from the center of the faith to the periphery. Because it is about "creation" he does not want to speak about sin and grace, that which is still the center of the gospel, but about other things. I will take them up from the last to the first. Grace-goodness, justice, power, presence of God, being-together with God. God is not alone. The human is not alone. God exists, the human exists, the world exists. One hears how Barth comes from the cross to the creation. Or really, he does not go from the cross, the middle point, but from the incarnation, thus, from the circumference of the gospel. But if one does that it is still the question whether one really goes out from the revelation in Christ to arrive at the creation. Now it is not from the center but from the two natures, not from the work of Christ. It is incarnation-creation....But the creation is a work and so one must go out from the work of Christ, backwards to arrive at creation. From grace as atonement—then one arrives in Genesis 3 and not in Genesis 1 and 2.[8]

Barth thus attempts, incorrectly, in Noordmans's view, to reason backward from Jesus Christ to arrive at Genesis 1 and 2, i.e., at created reality as such, as "form." But that can only succeed when one goes out from Jesus Christ as himself "existing reality," as "form," thus, from what he *is* (his "two natures," the divine and the human). But if you do that, you have chosen a mistaken starting point. Then you have let go of what is precisely the "center of faith," the core of the gospel, grace as atonement, brought into reality (accomplished) by Christ at the cross. Whoever would really, evangelically, go out from Christ in his thinking must not begin with what Christ "is" (in his "natures"), but with what he *has done*, with his *work*, thus not with the incarnation in itself, but with the cross. And then one arrives decisively not in Genesis 1 and 2 (or with "created reality" in itself) but in Genesis 3 (where we and our reality are typified as fallen reality, driven back upon the atonement.

[8]   *VW* 3:685f.

Previously, Noordmans had valued Barth's *Römerbrief* (see chapter 6) for the salutary-critical approach given there. It is true that he had, in that context, pled for a greater appreciation of new life in the Spirit. To his understanding, Barth had placed too much emphasis on the critical, the verticality of the Word of God and given short shrift to the work of the Spirit. But he now saw Barth's later, developed, positive-Christocentric theology (inclusive of a theology of creation) as a corrective in the wrong direction. In his view, this theology was certainly a theology of Christ but not a theology of the cross (and thus too little a genuine Christology).

CHAPTER 15

Mature Theology (2): *Gestalte en Geest*

The Spirit Who Shatters the "Gestalte"

We ended the previous chapter with a report of Noordmans's critique of Barth's doctrine of creation. This critique is different from and sharper than his earlier critique of Barth's *Römerbrief*. Still, there is a connection. This later criticism coheres with the earlier one in that in his judgment Barth has given short shrift to the work of the Spirit.

With that we have become involved in what was earlier noted as the second characteristic theme of Noordmans's theology, his vision of the coming and work of the Spirit as the real, decisive action of God to us and our world. He worked this theme out particularly in his *Gestalte en Geest*.

The title was chosen consciously. Noordmans understood "gestalte" to be the factual, existing reality, what is traditionally called "creation" (but what he himself would not call it!). And he understands the Spirit as God's judging, judicial power that enters into this existing reality, this "gestalte," critically and shatters it to form a new gestalte through the process of shattering—ultimately the reality of the kingdom of God. This judging, shattering action of the Spirit is, according to Noordmans, the real "creating," that "creating" that he qualified as "separating," "pulling apart" (already in his discussion of Gen. 1). For that matter, it does not remain in this state of brokenness; indeed, it is the transitional phase to the new gestalt. Noordmans called it "re-creation," and the Spirit the "Recreator." It is in the work of the Spirit that the future takes on a gestalt. We saw (in chapter 8) how he highlighted this in his book *Herschepping* [Re-creation] (which, also not accidentally, has just that title!).

In his meditations in *Gestalte en Geest,* Noordmans shows how matters unfold on this theme throughout the entire Bible. He meditates on various biblical figures, humans, "gestalts," who must go through the shattering. In the Old Testament they are, for example, Abraham, Moses, Saul, and David. In the New Testament, it is Jesus par excellence as "God's gestalt," the one who is foreseen in the Old Testament, in whom is summarized that which is present in the Old Testament only as broken pieces. Subsequently, in new meditations, Noordmans puts the peculiar work of the Spirit (the Spirit as "articulator of God's gestalt") on the agenda and thereby asks consideration for Paul, "the apostle of the Spirit."

Jesus: The Broken Gestalt Par Excellence

Most characteristic of Noordmans's position is his emphasis that Jesus' gestalt as well must undergo a shattering. Jesus is *par excellence* a broken gestalt, without form or glory. Most fundamentally, the gospel proclaims Jesus as the crucified. The gospel of his birth bears this same stamp. It certainly does not tell of the birth of a model human. As Noordmans says it in one of his Christmas meditations (on Luke 2:7):

> It was not the intention that Jesus would become human only in order to belong to our kind and then to show what could be made of the human. That he became such is not a compliment to us.... He has become human because we are the most miserable of all creatures....A human who is born does not remain what he is, like an animal remains what it is. So much happens with a human; he does so much, changes so much. And this all is articulated when one calls him *flesh.* It expresses not what he is, but what he has become: his weakness, his sin, his need, his death. For the sake of all these weaknesses, these sins, these needs, these deaths, Jesus has become human....He is born among the refugees. Among those

driven out of their land and condition, so that one can ask: are they still human?....Their fate appears stronger than their kind... Jesus...lies not in the crib as a model of humanity, but he lies there as a companion of all whose humanity has become problematic.[1]

Jesus, the broken gestalt *par excellence.* The Easter gospel does not deflect Noordmans from this theme either. One could think that if not the crucified, then at least the resurrected Jesus is the real, intended "gestalt," the new Human, on whom we must and may now concentrate. But according to Noordmans that too is a mistake. Reflecting on the Easter stories and texts, he turns against an Easter enthusiasm that forgets that even with Easter God's kingdom has not yet dawned.

One of the meditations on this theme (on John 20:6) bears as a characteristic heading, "The Mists of Easter." There Noordmans points to the remarkable contradiction between Easter *liturgy* and Easter *gospel.*

> The Easter liturgy gives the impression that Jesus' resurrection dawned on his disciples as a streaming summer's morning. Our Easter songs...break out in "halleluias"...As to the essence of the feast, that is certainly correct. But in the description of the reality, as the gospels give it to us, that is not so evident. The stories waken in us much more the picture of mists and clouds, which first must clear up before the full day can dawn.[2]

The first thing that humans catch sight of is a stone, a stranger, an angel, grave clothes. Consequently they react with mixed feelings.

> We read of gladness, but mixed with fear, of shuddering and unsettlement...of timidity and terror...of gloom...of confusion... tears...and doubt. And even when the sun breaks through, when Jesus appears to them, then it appears that Easter is not yet like a summer day. The Lord appears but immediately disappears again....The shared life of Jesus with his disciples in the forty days between resurrection and ascension was very intermittent and that is the primary characteristic of this short period in salvation history. This offers the...confirmation of what Jesus had said to them earlier: "It is better for you that I go away" (John 16:7). And Jesus had also then said why this was better. Otherwise the Comforter would not be able to come. The coming of the Comforter would be a better completion of his work on earth

---

[1]   *VW* 8:244.
[2]   *VW* 8:313.

than his own fleeting appearances on the threshold of time and eternity. The provision for a continuing bodily association with his followers did not lie in the plan of salvation. Rather, that body formed a hindrance to it. When Mary Magdalene fell at his feet, Jesus said that she may not hold fast to him. For further associations with his friends he must first have been raised up to heaven. He could remain with them and dwell with them only through the Holy Spirit.[3]

The "mists" with which Easter morning dawns continue, strictly speaking, to hang in the air. They draw back fully only when it has become Pentecost. "Until then a continuing association with Jesus does not go smoothly."And one may not consider, Noordmans says, this forty-day period an unambiguous period of salvation, of Jesus-in-our-midst. One has certainly asserted that in these forty days the disciples were equipped for their later apostolic office, and that thus in the church as a table communion around the apostles truly the kingdom of heaven would have come. In such a vision, the essence of the church would be the continuation of what had begun then, in those forty days. It would, Noordmans argued, come down to the fact that the kingdom of heaven would have had exactly sufficient time in those days "to spin itself into a mystery." But such a notion is in conflict with the character of the closing chapters of the gospels. In fact, the forty days are one great preparation for the ascension. In this entire period, Jesus is already active, breaking off this form of direct association with his disciples and "being lifted up" (John 20:17). In the story of the ascension we see the "mists of Easter" "forming into the cloud which withdraws Jesus completely from the sight of his disciples (Acts 1:9). Their expectation then is completely focused on the coming of the Comforter."

The Turn of the Spirit

Noordmans calls the "Comforter," the Spirit, the "interpreter of God's gestalt." Or also the "shatterer" of that gestalt, of every gestalt, including that of Jesus. Interpretation, too, is a manner of shattering. In his *Koninkrijk der hemelen*, Noordmans had commented on that. Talk of Jesus must at its heart be talk of his *work*. Well,

the Holy Spirit, so to speak, breaks the work of Jesus into pieces, just as the bread of the Lord's Supper is broken before our eyes, and

---

[3]   *VW* 8:313f.

he distributes the pieces in order that we would be strengthened by this food.[4]

This is the same thing, Noordmans said, that the Heidelberg Catechism does with the Apostles' Creed, with its twelve articles; each part is taken apart and to each an answer is given to the question, "What use is this for you?"

We have earlier heard Noordmans maintain that the incarnation does not continue, not even in the saints, in the liturgy, in the sacraments, in the church (even less so than in the culture). No, it is preached, "interpreted," and so comes to us for good. In *Gestalte en Geest* he strongly underscores how important this is, in his opinion. For example, in his meditation on Acts 6:13 (the accusation against Stephen), Noordmans reproaches those who still maintain (Roman Catholicism, e.g.) a continuation of the incarnation (in the church) with a return to a time before Pentecost. Then one allows no space for the Holy Spirit. Just like the twelve apostles in the first chapters of Acts,

> do not know what to do with the Holy Spirit. The confession of the *incarnation*...succeeded well with them. But they do not understand perfectly the art of breaking with the gospels after Pentecost to experience with the Greek congregation the full turning of the Spirit that Jesus had prepared them for. They prefer to continue with Jesus and extend the gospels.[5]

Standing over against the twelve (Peter and the other apostles) in the first church in Jerusalem, the "seven men," Stephen among them, were instituted to "serve tables" (Acts 6:13). Noordmans sees a clear distinction between the Twelve and the Seven. The latter succeed (according to the biblical story) in completing the "turn of the Spirit" away from the gospel (as a historical tale). And with and after Stephen that is also the case for Paul. They and their work form the real theme of the book of the Acts of the Apostles.

> Then it is not longer about the *incarnation* or its continuation, but about the *inspiration*, the divine breathing of the Spirit on all flesh, through which all things are made new. [6]

Noordmans concludes this meditation with the significant sentence: "Every *push to the foreground of the incarnation* is a sin against the Holy Spirit."

4   *VW* 2:536.
5   *VW* 8:370.
6   *VW* 8:370f.

To begin with the incarnation apart from the cross, that is precisely the foundational mistake that we heard Noordmans point out in Barth's doctrine of creation. Naturally there is a difference with what Noordmans notes as incarnational thinking within Roman Catholicism (the notion that the incarnation continues in the church). Still, Noordmans gives attention to an essential agreement between the two. Barth's doctrine of creation is also, in Noordmans's view, a form of incarnational thinking. Thus, he also deems Barth's doctrine of creation as having given short shrift to the work of the Spirit.

"Paul Comes and Peter Goes"

As was stated, Noordmans views the book of the Acts of the Apostles as primarily and really about Stephen and Paul—at heart about Paul—not about Peter or the "twelve apostles." The latter have known Jesus historically and are thereby handicapped. They wish to carry on with Jesus as he was before, and the church also wants to do that ever and again. But— Noordmans argues repeatedly—it is just that which no longer comes into view after Pentecost. The path of God's works is laid in a different direction. Stephen and his companions, and Paul above all, have understood that. So the real apostolate is not that of the twelve but that of Paul. Hence the motto by which Noordmans summarizes the intention of Acts: "Paul comes and Peter goes." That is another way of saying that in the end it is not Jesus but the Spirit who matters for us.

This is a crucial point for Noordmans. Rather than hold the notion that the Spirit belongs with Christ, one should, according to him, put it the other way around. In *Het Koninkrijk der hemelen*, speaking of the article of faith in the Holy Spirit, he said it as follows:

> One can say that the work of the Holy Spirit embraces that of Jesus Christ....Just as the entire work of mediation really lies in the article on the return of Christ and on the last judgment, so again is the confession of the Holy Spirit yet more inclusive.... The Spirit embraces the entire creation and re-creation. In the beginning it is the Spirit of God hovering above the waters (Gen. 1:2), already before the Word went out. And at the end it is the Spirit and the bride who say to the Word: Come (Rev. 22:17).—So he also encompasses the entire work of salvation and incarnation. Jesus is conceived by the Holy Spirit and he is replaced on earth by the Holy Spirit.[7]

---

[7]   *VW* 2:533.

In *Gestalte en Geest* we find this thought again in the meditation, "The Realism of the Spirit," on 1 Corinthians 2:10: "The Spirit searches out all things, even the depths of God." Noordmans underscores that it really is all things that the Spirit searches out. Not only the letter (which indeed may not remain a dead letter), but also the matter to which the letter points. The Matter, that is, Jesus, who is born, who has suffered, who is crucified, dead, buried, was raised, lifted up. It can "not be God's intention that these facts of salvation would possess a durability that would have made the continuation of salvation history at Pentecost impossible." It is also the case here that the Spirit searches out—evaluates—all things.

> The Spirit presses through not only in the letter, to bring it to life, but also in the matter, the fact. The fact of salvation as well, without the Spirit, can become as dead as the letter. The Spirit has something to do as well behind these matters. He must again search out the depths of God. He must know what God intends with these facts....We are left not alone with the facts that the gospel proclaims to us.[8]

The Spiritual Gospel in the Letters of Paul

The meditation just cited is one of a long series dedicated to Paul, "the apostle of the Spirit." From what was cited above we can expect that for Noordmans the main accent in the New Testament does not lie (as it clearly does in the tradition of the church) in the gospels, but in the letters of Paul. He highlights the fact that these letters are the oldest part of the New Testament, older even than the gospels. "The Holy Spirit has begun with speaking and writing *spiritually* about Jesus before the evangelists did so more *historically*." We must take cognizance of what that intends to say. "The foreign Jews and the pagans who have not known Jesus in the flesh and to whom the gospel tradition was slow in coming have received him in a sermon and in a letter."

Noordmans calls Paul's "main letters"—Romans, First and Second Corinthians, Galatians—"the four gospels of Paul." In his meditation under that heading, he goes into the difference between Paul's "gospels" and the other, well-known gospels, primarily Matthew, Mark, and Luke.

> One notes in Paul's letters little of the variety of events from the synoptic gospels....Paul never narrates stories of Jesus, other

8   *VW* 8:358.

than a short historic excursus which he gives to his message that Jesus was "given over for our sins and raised for our justification" (Rom. 4:25).[9]

Paul (more even than John) proclaims the gospel spiritually, not as story. That applies as well to his preaching of the cross.

It is a fact that powerfully appeals to fantasy, to the eye. These three *bodies* lifted up in the agony of death on the hill of Golgotha. It appears that at least here preaching must be *narrative*. But what do you think of Paul when he makes the cross audible in 1 Corinthians 13? The cross, on which Jesus does not seek himself and takes no account of the evil (v. 5); where he takes all on himself and bears all (v. 7). In this audible form the apostle has set the cross in the midst of the other gifts in the first Christian church; between faith and hope the greatest (v. 13), love....So Christ lives even *in* us....So the apostle can describe the cross in his own life when he writes, "...it appears to me that God has appointed us, apostles, to the lowest place, doomed to death, for we have become a spectacle for the world..." (1 Cor. 4:9). Can one find anywhere a more striking description of Golgotha? But now the hill lies also in the life of the apostle. To learn the love of Christ one can thus also read the four gospels of Paul; in the earliest days one had nothing other than these spiritual gospels.... When we hear the persuasive appeal of Paul in these letters, then it appears to us as if we hear the cooing of a dove. The dark, muffled tones are not made by the voice boxes of the bird alone, but the entire feathered creature trills the song. So Paul's entire apostolic existence vibrates as he writes these letters. And with him moves the love of Christ with whom he is one in the Spirit. And behind that the heart of the Father. Do you find that this spiritual, existential image of Paul is inferior in the face of the historical with the other gospels?[10]

The Future Character of the Work of the Spirit

Finally: does this mean a spiritualization of the gospel? On the contrary. We could better call Noordmans's theology—as theology of the Spirit—eschatological, future-oriented. We already saw how Noordmans points to the all-embracing work of the Spirit. That also

---

[9]   *VW* 8:408f.
[10]   *VW* 8:409f.

includes the work of the Father—creation. So, it can also be put the other way around. It is only in the work of the Spirit that we see fully what "creation" really is. And this is what creation is: the breaking through of the consummation. It is "re-creation," a new act of God, coming from the other side, from out of the end.

We recall Noordmans's expression, God "is much more the God of the future than of the past." His is "the Father from the kingdom of heaven." We recall (chapter 13) how Noordmans emphatically introduced the fact that the gospel is also the gospel of the beggar, of the poor, Thereby we remember that already in *Herschepping* (chapter 8) he brought just this "gospel of the poor" into connection with the work of the Spirit. That work is pronouncing judgments on our existence, justifying, creating judgments. All things receive a new predicate. All becomes new. Where the Spirit wafts, life comes again in the "valley of the dry bones" (Ezek. 37).

Life Completed

Gestalte en Geest was the completion of Noordmans's activity. When that book appeared, he had already laid down his pen. At the end of 1953, for reasons of health, he had had to cease writing meditations for *In de Waagschaal*, and there had been earlier periods of illness. Repeated notes of declining physical possibility could be heard in letters from the final years. Indeed, the power of the spirit continued unbroken to the end.

The Rotterdam minister, W. A. Zeydner, who had been friends with Noordmans for years, wrote in retrospect, "The final years were one heroic struggle against terminal illness."

Noordmans died in his residence in Lunteren February 5, 1956, at eighty-four years old. He was buried February 9 in Laren, the place where and from whence he had been active for so many years. In the preceding memorial service, in the church in Laren, Zeydner presided, together with the local minister, K. R. ter Stege. Words of thankful remembrance were also spoken by the synod president, the Reverend G. de Ru, and the church professors Haitjema and Miskotte, both of whom had long worked together with Noordmans and had remained in close contact with him.

In an *In memoriam* Zeydner wrote, "It is not given to us to elevate Noordmans to a 'church father.' But whoever reads Noordmans's book on Augustine understands that only a family member of the church fathers could so much be one of them."

INDEX